DATE DUE		
JUL 21 1997		
OCT 22 1997		
MAR 17 1998		
JUN 13 1998		
JUN 30 1997		

ALASKA BOUND:
A Life of Travels and Adventure in the Far North

Michael P. Dixon

Dixon Paperback Company

Alaska Bound: A Life of Travels and Adventure in the Far North

© 1996 by Mike Dixon.

Printed in the United States of America

Published by:
The Dixon Paperback Company
PO Box 240804
Douglas, Alaska 99824-0804

ISBN: 0-9639981-0-2

Library of Congress Number 94-093811

"The Alsek/Mt. Blackadar Expedition"; "The Great Alone: Mushing Dogs in the Arctic"; and "North to Alaska: Sailing the Inside Passage" were originally published in the *Salt Lake Tribune*.

"Fairy Tale: Kayaking Tracy Arm" was originally published in *Alaska Outdoors* magazine.

Every effort has been made to trace quotes and other material used in this work and to secure permission when required. In the event that any question arises as to the use of this material, we will be pleased to make necessary corrections in future printings.

The author wishes to express his sincere thanks to the following: Jonathan Bliss, Chuck Stotts, Colman McCarthy

North to Alaska, by Mike Phillips
Copyright 1960, Twentieth Century Music Corporation, renewed and assigned to EMI, Hastings Catalogue Inc. All rights reserved. Used by permission of Warner Brothers Publications Inc., Miami, Florida 33014

"The Second World War," by Winston S. Churchill
Houghton Mifflin Company
215 Park Ave So., Ny, Ny 10003

Additionally a special thanks is due to the following artists for their drawings and paintings: Peggy Kadir, Rod P. Dixon, Jerry Dixon, Jim Asper and other unknown artists.

Front Cover Photo: Alsek River and Mt. Blackadar
Back Cover Photo by Kim Turley and Jerry Dixon

To Meme, who in my dreams and real life
rescued me from the ice flows.

*Most authors came to Alaska and the Yukon,
declared it was God's country, and then left.*

— Unknown

CONTENTS

Maps of Alaska and the Yukon Territory
appear beginning on page 72

INTRODUCTION

I hate introductions, forewords, prefaces, prologues, etc. I never understood what most of those strange words meant any way. If you want adventure you jump into the middle of a book and read backwards; that way you develop a different perspective of it. You might not understand what you read, but at least you looked at it from another angle.

There stories were originally published as travel articles in newspapers and magazines. Someone suggested they would make a good series of essays and strung together they are adventures of twenty years in Alaska. Since the essays deal mainly with Alaska, there are some parts of the author's life which are not recounted here, but this tends to neither add nor distract from the story.

p. kadin

FAIRY TALE
1987

*He was alone. He was unheeded, happy, and near to the
wild-heart of life. He was alone and young and wild and wilful
hearted. Alone amidst a waste of wild air and brackish waters
and sea-hair vest of shells and tangled and veiled grey
sunlight.*

— James Joyce

Having deposited me and my kayak in the water, the cruise
ship pulled away on its fifty mile return trip north from Tracy
Arm National Monument to its home port of Juneau, Alaska.
I bobbed in the water in my inflatable boat staring at a hundred
foot wall of ice. Pieces would calve from the tidewater glacier
plunging down the face until they disappeared in a spray of ocean
which sent waves in my direction and kept me bobbing in the
water.

After I had sacrificed a roll of film to that icy giant, I turned
my one-man kayak towards an island I had picked for my camp
site. Nestled in the mountains with no name was an island with no
name located at the junction of two inlets each of which contained
its own glacier that reached the ocean. Both tidewater glaciers
were visible from the island. A single channel then continued on

1

fifteen miles to complete what is known as Tracy Arm National Wilderness comprised of steep granite walls and rivers of ice.

The glaciers snake their way to the sea through the coastal mountains that form the barrier between Canada and Southeast Alaska. Dark seams of crushed rock run down the glaciers as if they were freeway lanes. On the face of the glacier, the ice after a recent calving is as dark blue as a new pair of jeans. This is caused by the air being forced out of the ice and changing the refraction of light.

As I paddled my way towards the island I passed several icebergs in various states of melt showing ridges where the part exposed to the water melted faster than the part in the air. After too much melting, an iceberg would flip on its side or break in two causing more waves.

It was late in the day when the boat dropped me off, and I was feeling fatigued from lack of sleep the night before. I picked my way through ice flows and the milky green water rendered thus by suspended "rock flour" created by the grinding and rock crushing of the glaciers as they slid between the mountains.

I reached the island and found a site to disembark. I unloaded my gear and pulled my kayak up above the high tide line. Southeast Alaska is not known for its level spots because 20,000 years ago, during the last Ice age, the area was stampeded by a herd of glaciers (the glaciers in Tracy Arm are remnants of that last Ice age). Today everything is located in relationship to hills — whether it be on the side, top, or valley. The situation is even worse in these fjords as sides of mountains plunge a thousand feet perpendicularly without moving 100 feet horizontally. Up against that, I located my camp site on a ridge a few feet wide, because it was the only flat space. To roll over in bed meant to fall off of a cliff.

I dined on instant freeze-dried food which tastes as good as any steak as long as you are hungry enough. While I was having my nightcap and cigar (I can't camp without a cigar), I discovered that for a circumference of thirty miles (as far as I could see) I was the lone human. I was the fortunate ruler in a palace of ice in a kingdom by the sea.

Seals came to inspect the new arrival on their island, sticking their heads out of the bone chilling water of 34 degrees. How they navigated in that milky water was beyond me. Icebergs broke in two in front of me and wallowed in the ocean. Two eagles fed their young in a nest on the same island. Eventually, I grew too tired to appreciate

Kayaking *by Jerry Dixon*

all this and retired to my tent. It rained all night which is not unusual in the rain forest of Southeast Alaska. The ice giants were being well fed. Rain turns to snow in the high mountains and then into glaciers. I awoke at two in the morning because I had gone to bed early. As I gazed out into the darkness and rain I saw icebergs floating by the island like freight trains in the night. One iceberg the size of a hotel drifted past. I read while the rain poured down and I straddled a cliff in my tent hoping the wind would not blow. Then I fell again into sleep.

When I awoke in the morning, the ice giants were through dining and I anticipated a day of sun. That was the good part. The bad was that during the night the wind, current and tides had blockaded my island with icebergs broken off the glaciers. I would have to fight my way through the ice pack in a rubber boat – something similar to a balloon at a porcupine convention.

I packed my gear and headed to my previous place of landing which was now a twenty foot cliff because the tide was out. I found another spot suitable to launching a kayak, but the approach to it involved traversing smooth, moss-slickened rocks. I swore I was going to break a leg before I even had a chance to drown myself. After all my gear was stored in my rubber kayak, I re-inflated it with a foot pump. I lowered myself in, installed my spray skirt which kept water out and departed. Slowly, I picked my way through the ice flow with my double ended paddle. Several times I had to back track because the leads in the ice I had followed dead-ended. Many of the icebergs were as sharp as razors though more brittle.

At times icebergs broke in pieces and waves sent ice crashing against my boat. In a rigid kayak I would not have felt as much fear. With this rubber kayak I was deeply concerned. It would have taken some bad luck to sink me, but if I had flipped or sunk, that was it. There was no rescue.

I could not do an Eskimo roll in an inflatable kayak (too clumsy). Fifteen minutes in the water and you are unconscious and then dead. I had been in water this cold before in a ridged kayak, and after two Eskimo rolls my head hurt so from the cold I could not stand it. I made it, however, without any unfortunate damage to me or my boat. I was glad to have left that part of the trip behind.

The cruise ship picked me up on schedule and we headed back to Juneau early since the boat could not get through the pack ice to the glaciers. I saw a bear swimming the channel and I returned his crown to the true king. He snorted as if he always knew I was a pretender to the throne and kept on swimming. I saluted the lone sentry at the entrance to Tracy Arm, an eagle perched on an iceberg. He seemed more concerned about looking for fish.

As we left Tracy Arm new visitors were arriving. A film crew equipped with a hand-carved Tlingit Indian war canoe pulled into sight. They were there to film John Muir's exploration of Tracy Arm which took place in a canoe guided by local Natives. John Muir (the founder of the Sierra Club, a great naturalist and explorer) would later explore what is now Glacier Bay National Park also located in Southeast Alaska. He would have been happy to know that Tracy Arm had remained as he found it almost a hundred years ago.

4

As I departed the home of the ice giants, I was glad to know that fairy tales had not died with my youth. There are castles in the air though they be made of granite. There are dragons though they be shaped like icebergs. There are palaces even if of ice and there are enchanted lands and magical kingdoms by the sea.

p. Radin

ALASKA BOUND, PART I
1973

*A bunch of the boys were whooping it up at the
Malemute Saloon.*

— Robert Service

But the trip to Tracy Arm was in 1987 and I am getting ahead of myself. The story begins in Utah in 1973. My rationale for going to Alaska was simple: I needed money. More particularly, I needed money for law school. I could not make the money I needed in Salt Lake City, Utah for my first year studying law and swimming in the quagmire of paper. My going to school in the fall depended upon my monetary success in the Alaskan summer. The destination was Fairbanks.

I threw my gear in the back of a pickup belonging to a friend of my older brother's who was returning to Alaska to smokejump. This trip gave me the dubious distinction, in a four month period, of driving from Puerto Vallarta, Mexico to Fairbanks, Alaska, a total of 5,000 miles in five days (mostly over dirt roads).

Rad (my brother's friend) and I switched driving while the other slept in the front seat. After passing through Montana, the drive north was mostly flat plains, until we hit the mountains separating the MacKenzie River drainage from the Yukon. Outside of Whitehorse, Yukon Territory, I saw the finest display of northern lights I would see for twenty years. Green snakes slithered across the blackened sky. It was April and the total light of summer had not yet overtaken the north.

About 100 miles out of Fairbanks we both ran out of steam. We had driven 3,000 miles in three days and then stopped at Whitehorse, Yukon Territory for a couple of brews and twelve hours later we were both feeling the effects. I was too tired to drive, so I crashed against the truck door and went to sleep. Rad screamed that it was my turn to drive, but to no avail. His screaming must have awakened him, though, because he drove the remaining distance.

At Fairbanks I camped out at the smokejumper's station until I wore out my welcome, and then I rented a room by the week at a fleabag hotel in downtown Fairbanks. I had arrived in town with a hundred and fifty dollars which was quickly melting away. I decided not to stand upon my honor; I took a dishwashing job at a local hotel. In Alaska, even dishwashing paid well.

This was 1973, just prior to the construction of the Trans-Alaska pipeline. Around Fairbanks were stacked thousands of three foot diameter pipe for the pipeline which had sat idle for years while the battle for the Pipe went on in Congress. At that time Fairbanks had lost most of its log cabins to urban development but it still retained the flavor of the frontier. On Second Avenue were the most notorious bars, paralleling Anchorage's Fourth Avenue. A few years after passage of the Pipe, Fairbanks would be transformed, its population doubled. Many more cold steel buildings would replace the few remaining rustic cabins and houses.

I washed pots and pans for a month at night while I kept busy in the day looking for a real job. During this time I met other people who had climbed into the same boat I was struggling to survive in. Summer is the boom time in Alaska when the sun shines 24 hours a day and "daylight's a burning." Job seekers from the lower '48 flood the state and Alaska grabs up a good portion of them. This year was no different, and one could always get into a talk with some lost soul about job prospects.

Eventually I heard about a waiter position at an old time saloon located outside of Fairbanks. I procured the position, reported to work the next day and moved into my quarters behind the restaurant. There were a lot of things about this outfit that no one had told me when I was hired. The proprietor worked as a bartender in the saloon across the street from the restaurant and performed in skits and

Trees *by Jerry Dixon*

recited poetry by Robert Service. He worked as a carpenter in the lower '48 during the winter and had a degree in psychology. He was not a big man nor was he young, but he was not afraid to jump into the many fights that occurred at the saloon. Besides being an alcoholic and a sociopath, he was not a bad person.

On the other hand, his wife, who ran the restaurant (into the ground), was a former lady of the night and could out-drink her husband any day and usually did. At least the owner could run the bar which captured the past well with its sawdust and 1890's atmosphere. His wife did not succeed in this business, though she had been a success in her former one.

In the restaurant we served sourdough biscuits with no sourdough in them. We claimed to offer Shee fish which is a native fish of Alaska, but we substituted halibut. Our steaks were frozen solid a few minutes before they were cooked and, therefore, always came out black on the outside and frozen on the inside. It was the only place I have worked where I served the food and ran to escape the complaints.

When the health inspectors came, we were forewarned and hid the illegal and insanitary equipment in the back. The owner had a passion for seeing how far he could push the Department of Health. Each time the bar had a good night and multitudes of people jammed the place, the toilet would overflow because the septic tank was too small. The owner solved this problem by drilling holes in the bathroom floor.

The Fire Department told the owner he had to put up sheet rock between the kitchen and the hotel rooms above. The owner put up one sheet and then forgot about it.

The hotel rooms were another source of amusement. A person asked me once if people actually stayed in those rooms. I said I supposed they did, but I had never seen anyone stay there. Anyway, the restaurant did not serve breakfast or lunch and there was no place for guests to eat within a seven mile radius. They would have to walk, call a cab or drive seven miles for a cup of coffee.

The workers conditions weren't much better. We worked six days a week and were paid the miserable wage of two dollars an hour plus board and room. One bartender/waiter in the saloon stole hundreds of dollars a night to supplement his income and the owner was too drunk to tell the difference.

The food we ate was often spoiled and inadequate while the proprietor and his wife ate in their own cabin. We were seven miles from town with no transport and thus on our one day off we found it difficult to do anything. There was much unhappiness in the atmosphere.

One night I was over at the Howling Dog Saloon, which was close to the one I worked at, listening to the music and sipping a brew, when someone grabbed me by the shoulder and turned me around. My friend next to me jumped up ready to start swinging when, lo and behold, I recognized my dear older brother Jerry, up from Idaho where he had been smokejumping, to fight fires in Alaska. We smothered each other in brotherly affection and my friend put away his guns. Jerry and I and friends threw down a few brews and swapped lies well into the night.

Strangely enough, I was not to see my brother again during that summer because a series of events hurled me in a different direction. Possibly the appearance of my brother as a dashing smokejumper from the Salmon River, Idaho country was the cause for my change. But a few days later I hitch-hiked down to Mt. McKinley National Park, approximately 150 miles south of Fairbanks. On the way I met a person who worked at the Park and we hitched the last miles to the Park together. I had always wanted to work in a National Park. That day I rode the 80 miles up into Mt. McKinley National Park in order to see Mt. McKinley (or Denali as the locals call it) which was hidden in clouds (as usual). I talked with the bus driver about the Park. Something was churning inside me.

When I returned to the Malamute Saloon the next day by train to work at the restaurant, I lasted two hours before I quit. I threw my apron on the floor and walked out to the cheers of the dishwasher. I was the only waiter there and the dining area was half full; but the business did not fold on my departure in any case. I did hear years later that the wife was replaced as manager of the restaurant.

The day after quitting, I hitch-hiked down to McKinley Park and set up residence in one of the campgrounds. I wanted a position as a waiter and I was willing to camp on the door step of the Mt. McKinley Park Station Hotel until they decided they needed me.

While making my stand, I ventured into the Park again in the only means of transport — the bus — to the base of Mt. McKinley. Strangely enough I had never considered bringing a tent nor cover since I was from the desert state of Utah. I camped that night at Wonder Lake under a picnic table with my guitar and pack strategically placed on the cracks of the table to keep the rain off. A lady took pity on me and covered me with garbage bags. I would have made it as such had not a ranger thrown me out of the area into the bush saying the spot was reserved for those in a camper. I was too cold and confused to demand he arrest me if he wanted my removal. At least I would have had a dry place to sleep.

I wandered off into the bush with my plastic bags. I built a fire which was subsequently drowned by the rain. I climbed into my soaked bag which I covered with plastic garbage bags only to find that hoards of mosquitoes attacked any exposed flesh. Obviously these Alaska-size mosquitoes did not read the article I read which asserted that mosquitoes do not attack in the rain. I spent the next few hours in an outhouse smoking cigarettes to keep the bugs away, sipping scotch, and wondering what else could go wrong. Finally, too exhausted to stay awake, I stumbled to my bag and crawled in amidst the rain, garbage bags, and mosquitoes, and fell asleep.

In the morning I was rewarded for my suffering by what was to be my only glimpse of the great mountain. It was impressive, especially after a night of torture.

I returned to my vigil at the door step of the Park hotel and was eventually hired, mainly because I was the only person within a 100 mile radius who was looking for a job. I moved into the working quarters. The first morning, I recognized in the shaving mirror of the communal bath, the face of the fellow traveler from my hitch-hike to the Park the week before.

My roommate was a strange person with whom I spoke but three words in three months. I waited tables and made sufficient money to satisfy my greed. On the weekends I went camping but after several weekends of being rained out completely, I gave up the idea (it rained almost every day that summer).

Instead, the workers, who were mostly college refugees like myself, and I would borrow a truck from some fool and head off down the road to the nearest dance joint (McKinley Village) and dance up a storm. When we felt we had sufficiently impressed everyone with our dancing ability, we headed up the road in the opposite direction to Paul's Bar where we again did our Las Vegas routine. When we crawled home at 2:00 A.M., some of us went to work serving "tundra" breakfast to those tourists crazy enough to get up at 3:00 A.M. to see the Park in the light of the endless northern sun.

I fell madly in love that summer with the first girl who would have anything to do with me. Though I was too cheap to throw for a room to consummate the relationship, I was in lust. After dancing all night, we would sit in one of the lounges and talk. I can't say this was one of the happiest times in my life, but I have learned that if one puts oneself in impossible situations, generally one is so busy staying alive that there is no time to worry about one's problems. Thus did Alaska serve my purpose.

With September and the fall, law school was calling me to its bosom to suck my hard earned money out of me. I had to go. Being unable to decide my own fate, I figured law school could not be a complete waste (little did I know). I said good-bye to my tenuously held friends and my new love, most of whom I would never see again. The Park staff had enough of my greatness and had labeled me as a troublemaker who complained of the sub-standard living conditions and wages. They have my deepest gratitude for their decision which propelled me into richer endeavors.

I departed the Park with a few friends and joined the champagne campaign south to the lower '48. I had made enough money for a start at school. I went home to Utah where I threw my few belongings in my car and headed out to Spokane, Washington, and Gonzaga Law School to seek knowledge, truth, justice, and poverty.

p. kadin

ALASKA BOUND, PART II
1974

The day was done – One day of all my days.
Tomorrow would be another – And I was young.

— Jack London

I was back on the road. I had often known the feeling. How many times have I packed up my goods (everything I owned could be stored in a cardboard box) and shipped them to my mother's in Utah or stored them at a friend's? It was becoming routine now.

How slim was my wallet this time — only seventy-five dollars — in 1974 as I walked into the Seattle parking lot of the Alaska Marine Highway System after buying my ticket. I was cutting it a little short. The year before I had a hundred and fifty dollars when I headed for Alaska in a friend of a friend's truck. In Europe, when I headed out on my own, I had a hundred dollars; when I headed home to the United States from Peru, I also had a hundred.

It didn't look that bad and it didn't look that good. It was the next adventure: once more heaving myself into the abyss. I had just finished my first year of law school which is not the most memorable event in anyone's life. I was off potatoes after my senior year in college but now had to switch to noodles in law school. Pasta had been the main stay in our humble home where my roommate, Gary, and I constantly complained of being saddled with a poverty-stricken roommate who did not own a TV, stereo system or other luxuries. One good point was that we were both eligible for food stamps.

Putting oneself through law school is truly one of the seven tasks of Hercules, equal to cleaning out the Aegean stables. I had put myself through enough. The only thing I got out of undergraduate school was myself. I was tired of being poor and I was tired of noodles. I was going to go to Alaska and make some money and leave behind for awhile the laughter and frivolity of law school.

It was my second trip to Alaska. The year before I had headed out for the Alaskan Interior and Fairbanks. My previous employer, the Mt. McKinley National Park Station Hotel, had labeled me a trouble maker — somebody who complained about sub-standard food and living conditions — and therefore declined to re-enlist my services. While looking for a new job, I decided to explore new territory: Southeast Alaska was my goal.

I toured the Olympic Peninsula of the State of Washington with a law school friend who dropped me off at Pier 48 in Seattle, the southern terminus of the Alaska Marine Highway. It was a Friday and the weekly ferry left that night for Southeast Alaska, a place that had been recommended as fertile grounds for employment.

The Alaskan pipeline had been approved by Congress the past year; Spiro T. Agnew cast the deciding vote in the Senate. I wanted as much to do with the pipeline as I did with Spiro. They had enough oil on the North Slope to supply the United States for two years: what were they going to do, build a $10 billion pipeline every other year?

Southeast Alaska was as far away as I could get from the pipeline madness and still be in Alaska. I was like a trapper who, in the hey days of 1898 during America's Last Great Gold Rush, simply moved further back so he would not be bothered by the insanity. The pipeline paid great money for a short period of time, but gave no career: only early retirement with no benefits. The economic and ecological effects on the state were not much better.

It did not matter where I was going. The same scenario had been repeated so many times I called it the summer reruns. Each summer for the seven years since high school, I headed out to a new state or a new country. Consequently, I developed techniques for survival on a shoe string in strange environments. The first factor is to find a job, any job, that will keep the money coming while you find a real job.

Don't hunt for deer until you have established yourself on berries. Many people starve chasing deer with food all around. Never go to a state employment agency unless you are a veteran or have time to waste. This is especially true if you are an alien without a work permit or you are an out-of-stater in Alaska. Most Alaskans believe they are only loosely connected to the United States and extend their citizenship grudgingly.

The best way to get a job is by pounding on doors until they open. Go back and visit the same people and get to know them until they are looking for a job for you. If after six weeks you have not found a job, keep looking — it's a long swim home.

As I walked out into the parking lot of the Alaska Marine Highway, I was deciding I would not wait tables. It was back to the drilling rigs for me — mainly smaller core drilling rigs as opposed to oil rigs. I was determined to go back to the rigs until I saw the ship.

The ferry had arrived late that day, but it shone with bright lights in the Seattle night. Five decks high and 400 feet long, it was ablaze with light in the cool spring evening. It was my first close encounter with a large passenger vessel, and I was impressed.

I walked down the side of the vessel, along the pier, while cars and trailers were being loaded in the rear of the ship. The sides extended smoothly up past the car deck and staterooms to a dining room, cafeteria and bar on the boat deck.

Up one more deck, aft of the bridge, was a three sided enclosure which I later learned was the solarium. Hanging over the railing was a person in a white shirt and black pants. I wanted to rest on the railing like he did.

I shouted, "What do you do?"

He yelled back, "I am a waiter."

I returned, "I want that job."

We boarded the ship late that night: sometime after midnight (the ship, as mentioned, was running late). We shuffled around the ship like dogs circling before laying down. I was to remember parts of that trip distinctly even after many years.

While on the boat I asked questions about how to get a job on the vessel. Employees on the boat stated that on U.S. merchant ships such as this one you could not get a job unless you had a license to sail. You could not get a license unless you had a job. How anyone got to work was never explained.

15

On the second night out I had a regression. It might have been self-preparation for the great fear of that quantum leap of faith into the darkness. But I went into a black depression and I stood in a darkened corner on the aft end of the ship contemplating my existence. The next day I arrived in Ketchikan, my destination, and the voyage into the unknown began again. Maybe I needed to go to the depths of despair so I would know that whatever followed couldn't be any worse. The fear of the boxer is greatest just before he steps into the ring. Then he feels trepidation for what may befall him. But once in the ring he is so busy staying alive, he doesn't have time to worry. This was my worrying time before I stepped into the ring.

At 11:00 o'clock the next day we pulled into Ketchikan, and the bell sounded the first round. Ketchikan, the town proper, is approximately three miles long and two blocks wide. It hugs the shoreline like a snake following the glacier carved channels, which later filled with the Pacific Ocean, making Southeast Alaska all mountains and sea. Part of Ketchikan's main road is hung on a cliff.

The climate of Ketchikan is that of a rain forest which receives up to 13 feet of rain a year, making it one of the wettest inhabited places on earth. Ketchikan was, and still is, a blue collar town of loggers and fisherman. The two compete to see who can drink the most. Juneau the capital of Alaska, 200 miles north, offers largely white collar jobs. Juneauites drink a lot also.

I located the youth hostel and moved in with other denizens, most of whom were "between jobs" as I was. The hostel stood on pilings over the water like many buildings along the ocean front.

We cooked our meals on the floating docks in front of the building. At a dollar a day it was hard to beat. I immediately applied for unemployment and food stamps to keep myself alive and to avoid having to wash dishes.

I divided my companions, sleeping on the floor in sleeping bags, into the survivors and the non-survivors. The survivors were those who had readily sellable skills, such as logging experience, and those that were desperate (not easily turned away). I fell into the latter. The non-survivors were those who probably wouldn't make it unless a job fell on top of them. I was a seasoned veteran in this group. Inside I wore the decoration of the Five-State-campaign of 1969, during which I had seven jobs in five states in one summer. There had been the Italian front in 1969–1970 as well as the champagne campaign in France in 1970–71. I survived the drinking frenzy of the

Eugene, Oregon, battle in 1968–69 as well as being a member of the Peru in '72 Crew. Finally, the siege of Fairbanks of 1973 was still fresh in my memory from the year before.

I immediately started knocking on doors. Whenever I got half a favorable response from anyone, I always came back to chew the fat. In a drilling company office, I listened for hours to a person expounding upon the virtues of shipping gas via ships to the Lower '48. I wonder if he's still talking it up to this day?

I checked out drilling companies and waiter positions, including the Alaska State Ferry. In the ferry office, I was not encouraged to fill out an application. Summer workers are often regarded as foreigners who steal jobs from real Alaskans.

This is how one tells a true Alaskan: if you were in Alaska before someone else, then you are a true Alaskan and they aren't. The only problem is that this means there is only one true Alaskan and he is probably senile.

However, I continued to go into the Alaska Marine Highway office each day to try to fill out an application. After two weeks, I got my hands on an application and filled it out.

Each day I trekked through Ketchikan, going into offices and talking with people who were friendly and thought there might be a job for me. I had to go to the state employment office only once, when I first applied for unemployment. I filled out all the forms, which I had done many times, and which did not even increase my penmanship. When I asked the gentleman who was interviewing me to look up a waiter's job I had seen posted on the board outside his office, he proceeded to look up a job for me at Peggy's Drive Inn as a car hop for food orders in Seward, Alaska — 1,000 miles away. That was the last time I had any dealings with the employment agency. Again, only true blown-in-the-glass Alaskans were wanted, not outsiders.

My only other dealing with the employment office was when I was wandering the streets knocking on doors and decided to drop in and swap lies with some of the residents of the youth hostel. This was generally the non-survivor group that thought that the employment agency was there to help them. When I entered the office there were twenty people sitting in chairs in a semi-circle, all facing a man at a desk who received calls from logging camps for jobs. I too sat down and stared off into space to see if it got me a job. Few, if any, job hunters got out to logging camps this way. Generally, people sat in the office for two weeks before giving up and heading south without a job.

More resourceful people headed for the local loggers' bar, "The Fos'c'le," where loggers would buy them drinks at 8:00 in the morning and pass them twenty dollar bills to keep them alive. After spending several hours drinking in the bar, the job seekers staggered over to the local library to sleep it off. But some did eventually get work in a logging camp.

Once, while I was resting in the employment office exchanging war stories, two loggers crawled through the door stone drunk and were sent out to a logging camp because of their experience. Loggers are notorious for being transient and, like sailors are a vanishing breed of nomads. Loggers will throw a hot thermos at a tree saying that if it breaks they are going to quit, if not, they will stay. Others more definite in their plans might throw their hat in the air, saying as they do, that if it hits the ground they are going to quit.

The tales of loggers are numerous. When I first arrived in Ketchikan, I was passing the Fos'c'le Bar as a person flew through the door, across the sidewalk, with arms at full length for balance, then embraced a parking meter at three-quarters throttle which impeded his forward motion so that he melted to the ground around it.

Above the Fos'c'le Bar was a sleeping room where loggers took naps between drinking bouts. One time a logger was unable to get upstairs because the door was locked so he climbed up the outside of a building and went in through the window. He jumped on his friend for locking the door and scared him so that, combined with the liquor his friend had drunk, the friend went into delirium tremens and had to be hospitalized.

Loggers are not always known for their clarity of thought. On a street corner, two loggers were feeling rather bored. Suddenly, one turned on his friend and gave him a punch that sent him to the ground. The downed logger got up and proceeded to fatten the lip and smash the nose of his friend. Then they sat down on the street curb and roared with laughter.

In a logging camp one day, a seasoned logger noticed that a recent recruit to the outfit had a new pair of cork boots (special boots with spikes on the bottom) that were exactly his size. He told his friend, the camp boss, to fire the guy. After his boss released the new hire, the logger was able to buy a new pair of boots from the discharged logger at a reasonable price.

I was not interested in logging or fishing. Logging was, and still is, one of the most dangerous professions in America and Canada.

p. Radin

Each year 50 loggers are killed in British Columbia, Canada, and this does not account for the wounded and maimed. I don't shy away from doing physical abuse to my body for sport, but I draw the line when someone is making a profit off my injuries. Like a person who might give themselves freely to lovemaking but would never sell to the highest bidder, I draw the line when someone profits from my physical suffering.

However, after several weeks in Ketchikan eating beans out of a can on the floating docks, even prostitution did not seem that undesirable. One day a notice appeared for a helper's position as a puller on a commercial fishing boat. Having walked the docks for several weeks, I had come to know through conversation the various kinds of fishing vessels. This one in particular was a power troller that fished for prime salmon of the King and Silver variety that is served in restaurants and generally not canned.

Walking down to the boat harbor, I thought that I might enjoy going out on the protected waters of Southeast Alaska to fish although I had no experience at it. When I arrived at the boat I saw a member of the youth hostel group who informed me that the owner of the boat was gone but he had already filled the job which paid a percentage of the catch. I looked at the fishing boat which looked small even for the protected channels of Southeast Alaska. It appeared no larger than an overgrown canoe. From one end of the boat to the other were strewn fish guts and fish scales. Piled in the sink were dirty, greasy dishes from days (possibly years) past, and I knew the hired help was also the cook. Never had a boat looked so small. I was reminded of the riddle: What goes around the world but stays in one corner—a stamp. Well, the same is true of a sailor; he sails around the world, but occupies a space no larger than the boat. As I looked at the fishing vessel, it shrank in size. I knew myself well enough that I was not the type of person to go to sea in a small boat. The term at sea is "big boat people" and "small boat people" — small boats are more intimate — in large boats you don't have to see the same people all day.

I told the newly hired fisherman what a good job he had procured and how jealous I was of him. I showed resentment at his getting there first, but then wished him the best of luck. I assured him he would make a fortune with a fine canoe... I meant, ... boat, like that under him. He was smiling like a million dollars when I left. I never wholeheartedly pursued a fishing job after that. I knew myself too well. Far better to die a logger than to go to sea in a small boat and not only have to perish myself but take another person with me in an advanced case of cabin fever.

I saw that same person a few weeks later on the streets of Ketchikan. It had been a month then since my arrival and I was still under-employed. He had netted fifty dollars for two weeks' work. That had been enough high sea adventure for him and he was looking for another job.

About a month later, I again saw him on the street and asked about his occupational situation. He answered that he had secured employment in a logging camp several weeks back. I asked if he was logging why he was in town and not at a camp. He said he was in town because a tree faller had knocked down a tree which had let loose a rock that had sent him to the great clear-cut in the sky. Other than the 4th of July, the only time a logging camp shuts down during the logging season is when someone dies. The tradition has seen a lot of use.

I congratulated him on his new profession and wished him the best of luck. I saw him a month later with a cast on his right leg that came up to his hip. I was glad I had not prostituted my body to the logging industry but had instead gone back to waiting tables. Even when you get a job on the road there is no guarantee that you will live to enjoy it.

While I was camped out on the floor of the youth hostel, a woman moved in with several trunks. She piled them up in a corner and at night she slept encircled by them. She had dark brown hair like myself and was in her early thirties. I was 24. My luck in recent years with women had not been great and in a town with a large male population relative to female, I never thought of meeting women. However, with this girl who was not unattractive I engaged in conversation and presently a friendship developed. She worked for the Forest Service as a naturalist and was working in Ketchikan that summer at a local campground giving nature talks. She had worked on the vessels of the Alaska Marine Highway for many years as a shipboard Forest Service interpreter.

The first time I asked Jane (her name) out I went for broke. I put $25 on red and spin the wheel. We went out to dinner and I spent one third of everything I had.

The funny thing during this dinner was that I spent most of the time in the rest room. I had been on canned food for several weeks since leaving law school and I had not had any solid food until the steak that night. Possibly the steak went right through me. I camped on the great white throne for most of the meal. But a relationship had begun. It may have been a bad omen of things to come, but for the moment I had found a main squeeze after a long drought.

When the relationship was established, we needed more intimate surroundings. Sex with several people looking on was not our style. I was still unemployed, and my cash flow was quite small. She had just started work and had little money. However, she had access to a trailer where she did tours and had exhibits during the day. The trailer was located north of Ketchikan, inland at Ward Lake campground.

During the day the trailer showed how America's largest forest, the Tongass, was being clear-cut and turned into pulp for the Japanese at the cost to America of only $40 million a year. The display did not exactly say that but rather conveyed what a great deal it was. We got a pretty fair deal out of it as well. It had a nice carpet which became our bed.

At night, Ward Lake campground was a gathering place for teenagers. One night we huddled in horror in the trailer as drink-crazed teenagers tried to drive a car into the lake. They made it.

There was a certain amount of paranoia associated with that trailer. Every morning we awoke at the sound of any car.

"That's my boss," Jane would say. All our belongings flew out the back of the trailer into the bushes along with us. I lost a pair of boots in those bushes for several weeks because of such a departure.

Jane also had a van which was our means of transportation around Ketchikan. I had truly struck gold. But I was getting a little nervous because of lack of work. Many of the people who were first at the youth hostel were long gone — most to the south. A few had secured work. This summer had been a relatively tough one for me.

I ran the same route each day — I visited the same friendly people. Sometimes it was a fish cold storage. Other times it was a hall for drillers. Or I visited the drilling companies. One thing that makes an impression on employers is desire for the job. If you show up at the same place each day for six weeks, they figure you will stick with the job. I could feel bites and it was just a matter of time before I landed a real salmon (job).

I went to work one day on small core rig drilling test holes for a building foundation. This particular rig was a midget, but it brought back the times of working on core rigs on the mountain tops surrounding Salt Lake City, Utah. The problem was, I had fallen in lust, and being out in the bush on a drill rig was becoming less desirable.

One day I was hired by the Alaska Marine Highway. Somehow my application had slipped through the hands of personnel in Ketchikan and had made its way to Juneau where they hired me because of my experience as a waiter. Strangely enough, I was not called to work until a few hours before the ship left (I never received the message until long after the ship departed). Fortunately for the Alaska Marine Highway, there happened to be a local person at the terminal ready to go to work in case I didn't show up. It was the first time I had been hired and fired before I even knew I had a job.

Already fired, I saw that little could be lost by complaining. I bitched like hell in Ketchikan and Juneau and when the new flag ship of the fleet arrived at Ketchikan I went down and made my views known to the Port Steward who ran the Steward Department aboard the nine ships of the Alaska Marine Highway. Many crew members of the ship said I had only dug my own grave.

Three more weeks passed while I walked the streets of Ketchikan seeking gainful employment and watching the transients come and go; there was certainly a parade of characters through the youth hostel. One self-assured individual who was part Indian spent time with a fishing family trying to get out on their boat. He possessed a good deal of self assurance that I envied. I was to run into him over the years in Alaska. At times I saw his self confidence slip, but never far. Talking to me years later, he said he had made it out fishing, but, he had finally settled into leather work and lived in the beautiful San Juan Islands where he raised a special breed of horse.

This same person made a friend of a transient at the hostel who was one of the people who got along with everyone — another Jack

London without literary desires. He pulled in the diggings with a hard hat and a desire to log like everyone else. But he had the gift of gab and could make people want to help him. Before he blundered into the employment office and proclaimed that he had no logging experience, the denizens of the hostel informed him that he had to lie about his experiences as a logger to get a job. They told him of the terms to use, of logger lingo, of what to say concerning experience; they then proceeded to kick his hat around the room to give it the appearance of several seasons in the bush. He was sent out as a logger within the week, and I have no doubt that he made it as a logger. Whether he lived to tell his tales is another question.

Another person I met seemed to be an anachronism — a true conservative in the backwash of the liberal sixties and seventies. He had managed to bust into the purse seine fishing industry (a generally high paying fishery where they netted fish for canning with a net fashioned after a purse). He told me tales of working in a steel mill and bragged of how long he spent in a hospital because of his injuries — a true whore in my mind. He also told me how he had hitch-hiked from California to Prince Rupert, B.C., and then caught the ferry to Ketchikan. He said I had never done a thing such as this. Strangely enough, I did not relate that I had hitch-hiked across three continents (North and South America and Europe) by the time I was 21. I had to agree with him that I had not or at least I kept my silence.

Another fellow had been working in Prince Rupert, B.C., until they found out he was not American and ran him out. He later drifted from Ketchikan to Sitka where he went to work for the Forest Circus (Service). I was to run into him as well many times through the years. Such crossed trails are not unusual in Alaska because, though the areas are vast, the towns are small and people must use the same corridors of transportation through the towns. This particular youth hostel acquaintance introduced me to an old timer who was camped out on Ward Lake. One night we polished off a bottle of Jack Daniels while the old timer ran environmentalists into the ground. This same fellow lent us his fishing poles to mount an expedition against the fish though he later tried to leave town without repaying a loan to my friend.

Another person of the hostel floors was one of the most ill kept of all folks I have known. He never brushed his teeth nor did he like to bath or wash his clothes, but he had a cavernous eye for the ladies and they responded. One morning I awoke to find him in an epileptic fit and, having swallowed his tongue, he was desperately fighting for air. Somebody had the presence of mind to unlock his clenched jaw which allowed him to breathe. Once inhaling again, he came back to the land of the living. He said he had seizures from time to time and never bothered to have them checked out. He was a logger and eventually made it to a logging camp only to return after having another attack.

One citizen of the brotherhood of the youth hostel was a person with a pronounced stutter. I never found out if it came from childhood or his Vietnam experiences. I guessed the latter. He would stumble on a word for several seconds and then finish the sentence in the most self assured way. This person, after sitting in the unemployment office for several weeks, became tired of waiting and started shouting at the man who dispatched to the logging camp. He made it out to camp after that, but his goose was cooked before he got there. The loggers, having been notified by the employment office that he was undesirable, made it known to him that people can die easily from mistakes, some of which are intentional. He drifted back to town, showed up at the trailer one day and then drifted south, never to be seen again.

Jane and I spent our time, when not working or looking for a job, camping and hiking. We also raked for crabs at low tide and then boiled them over a camp stove (quite a job).

Cruise ships came to call at Ketchikan. Sitting out in the sun at Ward Lake while Jane gave a tour to the tourists off the ships, I wondered if one day I might be one of them. They talked of their aches and plastic knees and congratulated each other on making it off the ship.

Someday, years hence, I will come off of a cruise ship and see a young man in a park full of youth and adventure and fear and know that I was witnessing myself.

My luck had to break one day. It was a matter of odds and they were in my favor. I could feel the fish ready to bite at the end of the line. I could feel it attack the bait and hit it with his tail. My time was coming. Three weeks after being fired from the ships of the Marine Highway on which I had never stepped, I was rehired and assigned to the same ship to which I was originally dispatched. My future was made. On the same day I received two offers from two different companies to go out on drill rigs. But I choose the ferries which worked you week on and week off. I wanted to have more time to be in lust. Jane and I had since moved in with several other Forest Service people and we actually had a bed.

On the day I was hired, Jane was preoccupied with a car which did not run properly, but I could not get up the interest. We went out to a lake to celebrate, but she had to go back to town to straighten out the car situation. Again I was preoccupied. I was in nirvana. I had survived again. I had beaten the odds. Somehow I knew I would, but there is a great feeling of relief when one finally succeeds.

I sat on a log overlooking a lake chewing Copenhagen tobacco, slugging down beers and spitting at the world.

One night I gazed up at a waiter who rested on the railing of a ship in the cool of a Seattle evening. Two months later, on my second trip with the Alaska Marine Highway, I was dispatched as head waiter to the same vessel.

p. Radin

NORTH TO ALASKA

1974

How long does it take a totem pole to grow?

— An Alaskan Tourist

F our tiers of railing rise from the aft end of the cruise ship, each covered with people waving to friends and relatives seeing them off on their voyage to the 49th state and the Last Frontier. On top is the solarium, a three sided plastic enclosure that serves as the modern day steerage compartment where those who prefer the elements camp out. Dome tents spring up like mushrooms after a rainfall. The ferry is reminiscent of the days of '98 when miners and prospectors crowded aboard steamers leaving from exactly the same piers of Seattle headed for the gold fields of the Klondike. The main street along the waterfront and across from the cruise ship and the Seattle office of the Alaska Marine Highway is appropriately named Alaska Way.

The 400 feet long MV(motor vessel) *Columbia* pulled in this morning from Alaska, and its crew discharged 120 vehicles and 650 passengers, re-fueled, cleaned the ship inside and out, loaded stores, reloaded vehicles and passengers and is now ready to sail again twelve hours later. Every Friday the ship sails from Seattle to its most northern port of Skagway, Alaska, over a thousand miles away through the serpentine fjords of the Inside Passage and the terrible beauty of Southeast Alaska's rainforest.

In the dining room of the *Columbia*, business is slow as usual on each Friday night's departure. The new Alaskan visitors are too busy hugging the rails saying good-bye while in the bar, the long time Alaskans heading back to their gold mines, fishing jobs, logging camps, or the government bureaucracy are too busy swapping lies among other important things.

As the flagship of the nine vessels of the Alaska Marine Highway, the MV *Columbia*, pulls away in the twilight, the city lights are cut off at the dark water's edge. Hundreds of voyagers stare at the bright lights of Seattle which bid them farewell as the lights have done for over a hundred years to other Alaskan travelers. Most of the passengers are vacationers coming to see Alaska in the summer like those who took the first tourist vessel over a century ago. Everything changes, yet it all remains the same.

But some of the travelers are returning to their homes and some are looking for a new home and a new life. Half of all present day Alaskans were born some place else. Many came to Alaska on these vessels of the Alaska Marine Highway, camped out on the deck with nothing but a pack on their back, some dollars in their pockets, a few hopes in their hearts, and a dream in their head (as I did). Some people are running from something — either themselves or their past. Some people are running to something — adventure and a new life.

All the passengers have their dreams and hopes, whether large or small, as the ship plows the water of Elliott Bay destined for the thousand miles of protected waters of the Inside Passage and the emerald-green misty fjords of America's largest forest.

As the ship leaves the twinkling lights in the distance and passengers turn from the railings, over the public address system come the words from Johnny Horton's most famous tune:

> *Where the rivers are winding*
> *Big nuggets they're finding*
> *North! To Alaska.*
> *We're going north.*
> *The rush is on...*

In the morning, the *Columbia* coming up the Straits of Georgia approaches Seymour Narrows where Vancouver Island almost kisses the islands between it and the mainland, creating one of Canada's most scenic areas. Green and golden moss cover layers of volcanic rock in this magical passage less than 300 yards across at its closest point.

Large ships can navigate Seymour Narrows only at slack tide because the changing tide surging through the Narrows can flow like a river (up to 14 mph).

Leaving the Narrows, we sail over the remains of infamous Ripple Rock. The Inside Passage was created over 20,000 years ago during the last major ice age when glaciers cut deep valleys that were later filled by the sea. But at Ripple Rock the passage is partially blocked by the same volcanic intrusion that caused the beautiful layered volcanic rock of the Narrows.

Through the years, over 160 ships and as many lives had been lost on this rock. After several failed attempts to eliminate the hazard, the Canadian government in 1954 tunneled from the shore underneath the water up into Ripple Rock, and then detonated beneath the rock, the largest non-nuclear explosion to that time. The blast cleared the shipping lanes.

On the horizon, Johnstone Straits, the summer playground of the orca, or killer whale, comes into view. Many dolphins frequent the area as well, but the high back fins of the killer whales cutting through the water as a pod (group of whales) close in on a school of herring is what captures the memory.

The channel eventually widens, but the ever present mountains with snow-capped peaks dominate the skyline on both Vancouver Island and the mainland. Here the pockmarks of clear cut logging are easily visible. Generally, clear cuts of timber are kept off the major shipping lanes to leave pleasant scenery at the water's edge. How disillusioned some tourists would be to witness the ugly scars on the backside of what appears to be a pristine mountain wilderness.

At the end of Vancouver Island, the *Columbia* enters Queen Charlotte Sound, one of the few stretches of open water on the voyage to Alaska. The ship is forced out from the protection of the chain of islands along the coast. Being close to shore, waves bouncing off the shallow ocean bottom create large swells that rock the ship. These few open stretches of water remind us we are sailing the world's largest ocean, the Pacific; otherwise, the voyage is as smooth as sailing in a bathtub.

Further north is Bella Bella, the only town clearly visible in a 400 mile stretch of the Inside Passage. This native village of Canada is

p. kadin

serviced by Canadian ferries operating out of Vancouver Island and Prince Rupert, British Columbia.

The Inside Passage, a route of serpentine channels from Seattle to Skagway, is characterized by steep fjords carved by the last ice age. Glaciers still line the coast, a product of the heavy rain fall and the high coastal mountains. The climax or natural dominant growth for this area is mainly evergreen trees of spruce, hemlock, fir and cedar covering 90% of land.

The emerald green rainforest, with its ferns and golden moss, extends the length of the Inside Passage. Rainfall can be as great as 200 inches a year, providing streams for the salmon heading to their breeding grounds. Bears feeding on this rich protein grow to 1,800 pounds, almost three times the size of their inland cousins. Natives developed one of the richest cultures in all of North America off this horn of plenty. This is the land of the distinctive art of the totem pole and lodges.

Yet, interestingly, this land, though rich in food, is not over-loaded with population. Even to this day, civilization is just establishing itself in Southeast Alaska, where the tough environment has offered protection against the encroachment of both the Native and the white man. In part because of this, Alaskan Natives were almost alone among American tribes in never having signed a peace treaty with the U.S. government. Until recent times, there was so much land that no one wanted that there was no reason to have a peace treaty.

Because of the heavy rainfall, man's creations in Southeast Alaska which are not maintained, such as abandoned towns, simply vanish. The rain and occasional heavy snows destroy everything. Nothing burns — there are no fire-fighters in America's largest national forest (the Tongass) — everything rots away.

This northern rainforest is one of the toughest environments on earth for survival. Even the Arctic lessens in intensity after one deals with the Southeast Alaskan rainforest. In the winter, temperatures can fluctuate in a matter of days between fifty above with rain to seventy below, counting the wind-chill factor. Camping or working in those conditions often makes one wish they were in the Arctic with a constant 20 degrees below zero Fahrenheit.

It is a terrible beauty.

Twilight finds us in Grenville Channel, another narrow passage whose beauty is partially hidden by night. As we travel north the days become longer: in June there are 20 hours of daylight in Juneau. During the night we pass the port of Prince Rupert, British Columbia, the southern terminus for many Alaskan Marine Highway ferries. The Canadian port is linked by roads to the United States and is the northern end for Canadian ferries.

In the morning, the ship docks at Ketchikan, Alaska, called the First City because it is the first on the shipping lanes to Alaska. Some people call it first in rain because it receives 160 inches a year of liquid sunshine, making it one of the wettest cities in the world. Ketchikan lays claim to two parks featuring Native totem poles and salmon head up river through the middle of town. Long supported by logging and fishing, this town now is playing host to tour ships and tourists as Southeast Alaska becomes one of the nation's summer playgrounds.

The beauty of this emerald land and crystal blue sky is unparalleled when the sun is out and not so bad when it rains. The size and amount of fish a person can catch is staggering (50 pound salmon and 400 pound halibut).

Down the channel a piece is Wrangell, a logging and spruce mill town and the third oldest in Alaska. Originally Russian, it has served as the gate way to the interior up the mighty Stikine River that flows from the heart of Canada.

Leaving Wrangell, we enter the Wrangell Narrows: 18 miles of twisted channels with 56 green and red flashing navigational lights which at night resemble a giant pinball machine. Large foreign cruise ships don't even think about attempting this one. The largest passenger ships in this channel belong to the Alaska Marine Highway whose mates and captains know their ships and crews well and who pilot this stretch of water many times a week. The channel holds so little water that the void left in the water by the passing ship is filled by water rushing in which lowers the shore line as well.

Only once have I been caught bathing on the beach next to my homestead on the Narrows when a ship came through. I felt secure standing in the water up to my waist until the waterline dropped two feet and left me diving for deeper water in front of several hundred startled passengers. Afterwards, I rode the tidal wave back to the beach.

During the hour and a half trip through the Narrows, a great amount of wildlife is on display: bears, seals, deer, otters, and even some wild humans. With the help of the shipboard Naturalist, passengers often count over 100 white-headed crows (bald eagles) while in the Narrows.

At the end of Wrangell Narrows lies the fishing and Norwegian community of Petersburg which at one time claimed the highest per capita income in the United States because of its rich fishing fleet. Outside of Petersburg, icebergs are often seen which have calved off North America's most southern tidewater glacier, the LeConte glacier. This is a feeding ground of the Humpback whale up from Hawaii for the summer to feed on the plankton and protein rich krill (a small shrimp).

On its third morning out from Seattle, the *Columbia* pulls into Juneau, the capital of Alaska. Among its many attractions, Juneau has Mendenhall Glacier sitting in its lap from the huge icefield that half encircles the city. In the 1890s the capital of Alaska was moved from Sitka to Juneau because the federal government could not conceive of the capital being on an island, as Sitka was (Sitka, the old Russian capital, is visited by the *Columbia* on its south-bound voyage). However, until they invent highways that work well on moving glacial icefields, Juneau will continue to be an island on the mainland, encircled by water – half of it frozen.

Departing Juneau, the ships moves into the world's second longest fjord, Chatham Straits. The mountains start to close in as the

31

ship nears the end of its journey and the channel climbs out of the water. At Haines, passengers and cars disembark to head through Canada on their way to the interior of Alaska and such wonders as Mt. McKinley National Park. In the winter outside of Haines occurs the largest gathering of bald eagles in the world which feed by the thousands on the salmon run created by a warm springs in the Chilkat River.

At noon on Monday, two and a half days after leaving Seattle, the *Columbia* arrives at Skagway, the main jumping-off point for the gold seekers of '98 on their way to the Klondike during the Last Great Gold Rush of North America. Skagway has kept well the flavor of its historic past.

Here the last cars disembark to head over the pass into the Yukon Territory. A few brave people departing the ship who are long on tires and short on adventure may drive the Dempster Highway to the Northwest Territories and to within 70 miles of the Arctic Ocean.

By the time the *Columbia* leaves Haines on its southbound leg, the car deck is packed again with RV's and automobiles, and the ship is full of tired voyagers who have been traveling the state for weeks. The only real difference is that whereas in Seattle the vehicles were relatively clean, these RV's and cars show the dust of hundreds of miles of dirt roads.

The difference in the passengers is more subtle. People from the lower 48 now have become adjusted to the higher Alaskan prices and find the prices on the *Columbia* refreshingly low.

But more importantly, there is a warm alpenglow in the tired but happy eyes of these voyagers. Many travelers will mark well this page in their book of happy memories. And for some — well, they have become like myself. There is no reason to go home when you are already there.*

---

*The southern terminal of the Alaska Marine Highway system moved 90 miles north to Bellingham, Washington in 1989.

p. Radin

TENAKEE SPRINGS: THE ONCE AND FUTURE TOWN

1975

No one thing is true; it's all true.

— Author Unknown

Having secured a job on the Alaskan ferries, I was convinced by Jane that we should try homesteading in a little community called Tenakee Springs located ninety air miles west of Juneau.

I had decided to remain out of law school for a while, and we headed to Tenakee where I could still work the Alaska Marine Highway's week on and week off schedule.

Have you ever lived in a town where the proprietor of the local restaurant gets angry at you if you don't eat all your food? Where the person in town who owns cabins will not rent them? Where the person who was arrested for fishing without a license is the Chief of Police? Where the person who set fire to his boat and blew it up is the Fire Chief? Such is Tenakee Springs, Alaska.

Few places serve a better plate of food than the local restaurant (would you believe fresh not frozen french fried potatoes?), but never order food and not finish it if you expect to eat there again. The owner of the greater part of the town rents some cabins but most are in disuse for no apparent reason except that he probably thinks there are enough people in town as is. For him, growth for the sake of growth is a cancerous idea. The Chief of Police was not chief when he was apprehended, but he is now. He holds the distinction in Tenakee as being the only person to be recorded in *Ripley's Believe It or Not* to have fallen 150 feet out of a tree and lived to sue about it. The Fire Chief was not chief when he blew up his boat, but he is now. Maybe there is a pattern emerging here?

Tenakee is the home to many loggers, and I have seen how tough they are. One day a bushler (tree faller) was talking to me, if you could call it talking, because half of his face was swollen to twice its size. Apparently, he had been cutting limbs off a tree which had fallen across a gulch about twenty feet above the ground. He cut one limb which let loose another that hit him in the face; he fell 20 feet to the ground where his saw landed on top of him.

As I was talking to him he pulled a piece of wood out of his gums an inch long. He smiled and said, "Well, that's good news. I thought I had lost a tooth." He is afraid of dentists. He is not afraid of falling trees or falling out of them but you have to hog tie him to get him into a dentist chair. One time he finally had to go to the dentist because of a tooth ache. The dentist casually asked him which one it was since there were a lot of candidates.

Down at one end of town is Mrs. White's place with 50 cats. It is built right next to a house with 14 dogs. The two houses are connected and separated by only one door. It has been the desire of half the town to get that door open. Mrs. White is an elderly person and a live-in, taken care of by Lee Gault and his wife who live next door. Lee hunts the cats to keep their population down and has scored 123 so far.

One day I was walking down the trail when I saw Mrs. White trying to coach a cat into her house by saying, "Here, kitty, kitty." When that did not work she stepped behind the cat and the little old frail woman kicked it in the rear and said: "Get in there you dumb son-of-a-bitch before that bastard gets you." And there was Lee underneath the steps grabbing for the cat.

Some of the houses in town are built on or partially on the public road or rather the public trail. If you need more land, just

p. kadir

build on one of the trails. Right now they are erecting the firehouse on "D" street; not next to it — on it.

There are no taxes in Tenakee, neither land nor sales. However, it does have a several hundred thousand dollar boat harbor, a hundred thousand dollar school (recently replaced by a multi-million dollar school for twelve kids and three teachers), a fifty thousand dollar airplane float, a fifty thousand dollar television and telephone hook up by satellite (which unfortunately knocked out the radio reception), a hundred thousand dollar trail system and park, and Tenakee is now getting a three hundred thousand dollar dock for the ferry so that soon a seven million dollar ferry will come in. Also, there is the new Senior Citizen Center, the health center, and the new electrical system. You could ask the mayor where it all came from (because he had a hand in getting most of it), but he does not live here very often.

Tenakee Springs gets its name from the free hot springs bath which is the reason that the Finnish people settled here at the turn of the century.

35

So where is Tenakee? If a person tried to drive there from Juneau he would drown. If he tried to walk from the nearest town he might make it in two weeks. Sometimes a person can fly there or go by boat. Tenakee is in Tenakee Inlet where the brown bears out number the people and white headed crows circle in the sky. Salmon fill the streams and Alaska Pulp and Lumber has not cut down all the trees but it is trying. It is a place where no clocks read the same time and there are no cars to get the dogs out of the middle of the trail. A place where people back bit each other into the ground and then turn around and come up with $450.00 in a matter of hours to send a wife down to stay with her husband while he is in the hospital in Seattle. And these are not rich people but retired folks living on pensions and young people trying to make a buck logging or fishing.

It is a place where you can sit down in the middle of the trail with a couple of cases of beer and give a get well party to a departed friend and by nightfall half the town is there drinking with you. It is the last stop for old timers who have come to swap their last lies and drink their last beer before heading out for that homestead in the sky. That is Tenakee; lost somewhere in Southeast Alaska among the deep blue waters and the twisted hemlock trees and still hiding from the benefits of civilization.

It is the Once and Future Town. It is the "once" town because it is fifty years behind other U.S. cities. Yet, it is the "future" town, because some day the rest of America might catch up to it.

p. Radin

THE DEMISE OF
"GIVE'M HELL" BELL
1976

This out of all shall remain.
Those who have lived and have tossed.
So much of the game will be gain,
Though the gold of the dice has been lost.

from *"Love of Life"* — Jack London

One day up at my cabin site in Tenakee Springs, Alaska, a friend who was helping me build my cabin said to me: "Old Jim Bell was up here the other day saying he would be willing to help you with your cabin, but the best thing he said he could do for you was to lay a hammer up along side your head."

I smiled and retorted: "Yeah, that sounds like Bell. About a week ago he said he came up to the site and found you screwing around with those ropes and pulleys for the cable line to haul materials up to the cabin. He said that he arrived just in time, because in five more minutes you would have hung yourself."

Jim Bell was always short on compliments, but long on opinions and that is the reason I liked him. Because he never gave a damn what

37

anybody thought of him; to the very last he was his own man.

Bell was born in 1898 on Prince of Wales Island located in the rain forest of Southeast Alaska and near Tenakee. He said the fishing village of Craig was named after his grandfather and Bell Island with its famed fishing resort was named after his great uncle. Adventures of Jim have been recounted in a book written by his sister Margaret Bell, called *The Pirates of Icy Straits*, although in later years they were not on speaking terms.

Jim was 75 when I met him in Tenakee, a small, isolated, fishing village in Southeast Alaska and the place he had come to retire. He was six feet tall with a small paunch but his legs looked like those of a young man. His standard dress was a khaki shirt and pants. Though he wore glasses, his hearing was excellent. His snow white hair was thinning and was often covered by a khaki colored cap. He had buried his third wife six months before I came to Tenakee. People related to me how he would stand on the porch of his home and talk to people but would never be far from his wife who was dying of emphysema.

After 75 years of traveling the world Jim had come to retire in a one room building with all his possessions not worth over two hundred dollars and to live off social security and veteran's benefits. To some people that may not seem like the pinnacle of success, but Bell's wealth could not be put inside a wallet. His wealth was in his slow walk down the main trail of Tenakee telling people what the weather was going to be like and shouting his opinion of loggers and how they were about to destroy Indian River, a scenic area close to town.

Many times I have met old people who had nice homes with grandchildren running around them and yet they felt unhappy and neglected. But Old Jim did not have but one known relative alive (his other sister in San Francisco) with whom he associated, yet he never had any regrets and never felt sorry for himself. It moves a person to see a man of 78 (his age when he died) with nothing in his pockets but lint still get a kick out of life.

Yet there was more to Jim Bell than these things that moistened my eyes when he died. Rarely does one meet a person who holds himself in highest esteem. Most people need the artificial supports of position, money, friends and associates to bolster their image. Without these props, they melt away into insignificance. Not Jim Bell. Though he lived in a one room building, Bell never placed another person one notch above himself. To Bell, everybody stood upon equal footing, and nobody escaped his opinions if he felt like expressing them whether he addressed them to loggers or high officials in government.

It was on board the passenger vessel MV *Columbia* that I ran into Jim Bell as he was letting loose on my boss, the Port Steward, for the way the dining room was run (I was a waiter on the ship). Most people might have been intimidated to address the person in charge of food and room service on the eight cruise ships in the Alaska Marine Highway System, but not Old Bell. In the end, Jim was invited to lunch by the Port Steward and his wife, though he never changed his opinion.

Jim was on the City Council of Tenakee. People said he was elected because he told the big guns in town where to step off. Jim was the only member of the City Council who openly supported my federal homesite land claim against other members of the Council who were trying to run me off my land claim by claiming it for the city. Without Old "Give'm Hell's" support it would have been a much tougher fight.

One of the stories I like to tell is about when Bell and the boss from the logging camp were having it out in the middle of Tenakee's main trail. After a few short but pointed words, the two men parted and Bell was heard to say: "If those idiots can't put in a logging road down at Ten Mile Spit (which was another route to the logging site that did not go through town and up Indian River), then I'll go down and show them myself. I'll be a son-of-a-bitch if those bastards will get into Tenakee and build a road up Indian River while I'm alive." In the end they did not, because "Give'm Hell" Bell died one month before Alaska Pulp and Lumber bullied Tenakee into letting them into Indian River.

Bell's stories were lightening and fire to the kindling of my young imagination. He talked of shipping out of Seattle on square-riggers (sailing vessels) bound for the South Pacific; of trapping in Glacier Bay; of mushing from Barrow, Alaska with a dog team to Fort Yukon in order to spend Christmas with a lady friend; of fighting in Mexico before World War I and of having a ship blown out from under him during the first great war. He also recounted such romantic adventures as hiking from Stewart, British Columbia to Lake Atlin, a distance of several hundred miles through roadless mountains, while prospecting for gold during his summer vacation from the University of Washington.

Jim "Give'm Hell" Bell in Jim Bell Park, Tenakee Springs, Alaska by Jim Asper

He never graduated from college, saying organic chemistry got the best of him.

Some people say he never did those things and that the most he ever amounted to was a dishwasher. Maybe its true, but I know people who have done things similar to what Jim claimed and when they tell their tales, generally they get the look that people used to give Jim when he told his. In the end, it is not important what others think of you; only what you think or believe of yourself.

Jim had few regrets in his life. One day he discovered his first wife in bed with another man. He told the guy to stay right where he was; no one ever got what was not given to him; he picked up his gear and never saw her again or the son he left behind. That was until fifty years later when his son finally ran him down. All Bell could do was laugh and say he could never understand how his son found him. His son was also retired when they met four months before Jim's death.

Bell never had many male friends and he openly admitted it. But the women adored him. Every good looking girl that came into town seemed to end up on Bell's porch drinking wine with him. He set the rules when they came to his place. As long as they stayed off his bed they were safe, but if they did not then they were fair game. Bell raised marijuana in his home. He said he did not smoke much of it himself but he used it as bait for any young women in town.

Jim lived as if he would die tomorrow and yet at the same time he lived as if he was never going to die. Right up until the end he was smoking and drinking and chasing women as if it were his first time and might be his last. When I came back from wintering over in Juneau one year, he jumped on me for not getting a grubstake[0] for a fishing boat. He said he could get a Veteran's Administration loan if he had two thousand dollars, and he had found a young lady who wanted to be his puller (helper). He never stopped living and dreaming. He had palsy so bad that his hands shook like leaves in the wind, yet he borrowed my guns to go hunting. He had inner strength that paralleled the wilderness harshness in that both were unrelenting.

He died standing up as he would have wanted it — a heart attack just before going to bed. He would have hated lingering on in a hospital. When I heard the news I cried for hours. You never know how much you like a person until he is gone. But I knew what Old Bell would have wanted. I went to the liquor store, bought two cases of beer, sat down in the middle of the trail (no streets or cars in Tenakee) and started drinking. Soon people came by and stopped. Ace Boat Building, the local band, brought out the guitars. After the town meeting during which they named the park below my cabin site after Jim Bell, the rest of the town joined in. The liquor store opened up and was selling fast. By three o'clock that morning a good part of Tenakee was drunk. Most of the loggers never made it to work the next day -- just the way Bell would have wanted it.

I think the best thing Bell ever did for me and maybe Tenakee as well was to impress upon us his attitude towards life. Some days when I would come down from my cabin site after working all day carrying material 300 feet up a thirty percent grade through a rain forest to my homesite (in the end I hauled forty tons on my back), I would see Old Bell wandering down the trail at 78 and still happy and glad to be alive. That is when he helped me the most. If he could be happy at his age and in his situation then I could not see a reason why I could not be, too.

If a person could choose the way he wanted to die I wonder how Old Bell would have wanted to go. Myself, I would have liked to see him get into the fishing boat we never had a chance to buy and head out one stormy night, saying as he left for the last time: "I think if I can get up enough speed I can ram that log float down by Indian River and by morning in this weather those logs will be scattered and they will never recover them. Maybe we can run those loggers out of business." The next morning I would wake up and see logs scattered throughout the inlet and little boats full of men trying to round up the few that did not get out into Chatham Straits and were gone forever. If the dream went on, that night I would sit in the bar listening to what the loggers had to say:

"But that is impossible," said the first logger.

"I tell you that is what I saw," replied the second logger.

"Just what the hell did you see," asked the third logger.

"I saw Bell on a log. He was twisted up in the cable."

"We know that. We pulled him off it. But what is this other bullshit about the hand," demanded the first.

"Well, when I first pulled up, I thought it was another log. Then it rolled over and there was Bell all messed up in the cable and lying on his back. His arm seemed to wave each time the log rolled. It was like I saw in a movie. What's the name?"

"Moby Dick," I said.

"Yeh, yeh that's it. Just like Moby Dick. And his arm was waving like in the movie, but his hand was in a fist. Except, except…"

"Except what," said the third.

"Except his middle finger was extended. That bastard. I swear his middle finger was extended. You saw the smile didn't you? That was still there when you got there. Wasn't it?"

"Yep," said the third, "he was smiling alright."

But that is just a dream.

John Donne said it but I never understood it until the day "Give'm Hell" Bell died. "Ask not for whom the bell tolls" is what he wrote and I know it does not toll for Jim. I am sure if there is an after life, Old Jim is up there giving the Almighty the riot act because there is not enough wilderness in heaven and wondering where all the girls are. The bell does not toll for Old Jim. It tolls for me and Tenakee.

p.kodin

HOMESTEADING IN ALASKA: THE NIGHTMARE LIVES ON

1974–1984

Anything worth doing is worth overdoing.

— Jonathan Bliss

Homesteading in Alaska is a once-in-a-life-time experience: you only want to do it once. I felt lucky to have done it and survived. But to have the perfect homesteading experience, like a gourmet dish or a great drama, one must have the right ingredients.

The first item is a man on the run from law school. This person is desperate and will do anything to escape the ever-closing claws of reality. Such was myself. I successfully completed my first year of law school in 1974 and felt as good as a person with a broken leg. Living on food stamps was not so bad, but the law made me physically ill.

An important part of this epicurean delight is that the fool ... I mean adventurer ... must not know anything or little about homesteading in the Alaskan wilderness, building a house, etc. The more the person knows the less the drama and self-discovery and thus the less entertainment. Again, I was made for the role not knowing how

43

to run a chain saw, much less build a habitable dwelling in the wilds of the Far North.

The next spice to a successful homesteading is the setting. In my particular case, the sight was a little Southeast Alaskan fishing village with no roads but a free hot springs bath. To develop the plot, I had to perpetrate an act that would offend deeply the inhabitants in this Southeastern Alaskan community of 100 people (mostly retired). A drama of the first water comes from nothing less than walking into a stranger's house and defecating on their table. Therefore, in this town hugging the shore of an inlet of the Pacific Ocean, I settled in the town's watershed area above the community and declared my intent to build a cabin; homestead the land (get it for free from the federal government); and live in the area from which many people got their drinking water. Immediately, the possibility of endless conflicts springs to the forefront.

However, with any good gourmet meal, the dish is never done until properly sautéed or cooked. The bomb was there but someone had to ignite it. Fortunately, I had unconsciously made all the arrangements for this in advance. The key here was the woman who brought me to this Southeastern Alaskan paradise. Her name was Jane. I cannot take all the credit for this modern "Have Chainsaw, Will Travel." She deserves some small mention.

The first year of homesteading in Tenakee was enjoyable. Jane and I were amicably building a cabin and our foes had not yet mobilized against us. However, when I put my hand through a mirror and the ⅜" piece of glass shelving behind it, after a few glasses of wine and a disagreement with my beloved, this was a warning sign that not all was copasetic. The relationship went flat and lost its fizzle after a year in Tenakee when I could not marry a woman who could move me to assault mirrors. The hospital bills were too high.

After the plug was pulled on the romance, I stayed on in the town to work my land and build my house. Jane gave me a year to come to my senses and re-declare my love for her. But when I would not realize what a great love I was losing, she decided to kill me. She attempted this mainly through a drunken logger in town whose life had reached such a low ebb that killing someone did not seem that unreasonable to secure the love of this fair damsel.

When the curtain fell at the conclusion of this first act that could only happen on television and in real life, the logger discovered that killing people to show a person's love went out of style with King

Mike Dixon (right) and younger brother, Todd, on Dixon Homestead #1 in Tenakee Springs, Alaska–by Jim Asper

Arthur and the round table. But the logger deserves praises for his well executed performance because afterwards I didn't sleep for three weeks.

With no loved one to torture me, I had to become more creative to finish the final acts (Jane went on to love other victims). Every tragedy needs a second nemesis in case the first cannot survive the whole play.

Being the resourceful person that I was, I delved deep into my past to bring true pathos to the forefront. I knew some day I wanted to be a writer and that good writers write best when writing from experience. I had a true drama unfolding that could equal *Gone With the Wind* if made into a movie, or *War and Peace* if put into book form. I could not deny myself a future as a brilliant writer by letting this part of my life have an "Ozzie and Harriet" happy ending. Opportunity knocks but once (even if it killed me).

Besides, it was time to clean house and get the skeletons out of the closet. I was running out of room for my hang ups. I hope some day the town will forgive me for being chosen as a dumping ground for the nuclear waste of my overheated emotional past. But then no one ever said life was fair.

To put the finishing touches to the second act, I went to the well of my inner strength and brawn to manually haul in 100 logs and dig a complete foundation and pour it all by hand. My friends affectionately called me: "Mike the masochist." The philosophy behind all this is similar to hitting yourself on the head with a hammer: it's so nice when it stops!

When the pain and the suffering were still not enough to meet my psychological needs to destroy myself, I invented new exercises in futility, such as building a three story, double-walled, log structure of over 2500 square feet. Building in a primitive setting is difficult enough, but it is made worse by having to transport 40 tons of material to the building site on one's shoulders 100 yards up a 30% grade through a rain forest over ground littered with debris. As a friend once said: "If you are going to New York, there is no sense getting off in Chicago." Besides, it only took ten years.

I do not feel this story encompasses the psychological underpinnings for this dinner theater with the macabre. But if you have to go crazy, do it where there are only 100 people whom you will probably never see again.

I finally was making progress when I collapsed from exhaustion; became "bushed" or paranoid and felt I had to kill my tormentors before they killed me (such as the logger); and became so fatigued that I could no longer figure out ways to torture myself.

There may have been a happy ending to this anorexia's gourmet delight had I not been the resourceful person who has always made my life as difficult as possible. When I finally received title to my land after eight years of battles and paper wars with the city, surveyors, federal bureaucracy, loggers, girl friends, personal phantoms, etc., I decided that I had to show the town leaders as well as myself that I could still ram my head against a brick wall better than anyone else. I had to prove to the city council how tough I was by making sure it had at least one more chance to beat my brains into the ground.

I accomplished this by subdividing my land into two lots. At last, I managed to unite a good portion of the town against me and I no longer felt neglected and unloved because only a handful of the townsfolk wanted to see my body floating in the bay. This last ingredient provided the coup de grace for this Ghandi-esqe feast and was the last act in this "made for the legally insane" TV series. I subdivided my land and sold my house while they were still boiling the tar and tearing apart pillows for the feathers. As some one once said, "If they are running you out of town, get in front of them and act like it's a parade."

Not everyone will be able to enjoy homesteading as much as I did; nor will they reach the level of self abuse. But with the right ingredients such as hard work, the love for tragedy and a lose grip on reality, anything is possible.

p. kadin

LOST IN LAW SCHOOL
1978

Having burned out on my homestead and on ferries I decided to try law school again. It was time to do something different even if it was wrong. My greatest accomplishment from those years follows.

The Slumber of Sam McGee
Adapted from Robert Service

There are strange things done under the fluorescent sun,
   By the people who study the law.
The men's john holds its secret yawns
   that would make the ABA's blood run cold.
The students at night have seen queer sights,
   But the strangest they ever did see
Was the night in Labor law, when the professor saw,
   The slumbering Sam McGee.

Now Sam McGee was from Tenakee, up where the salmon heads for the sea.

Mike Dixon–Artist unknown

And why he left his home in the wild to study the law knows
    only the Lord,
For he was always bored, but that land of books seemed to
    hold him like a spell
Though he would often say in his sleepy way that he would
    sooner be sailing the swells!

On a January night we were caught in a fight over nuances of
    the law.
And talk of the boredom, though the students implored him,
    the professor all but ignored them.

49

If our eyes we closed then we began to doze, and some fell
out of our seats.
It wasn't much fun but the only one to whimper was Sam
McGee.

And that very night, as we sat packed tight in our chairs all in
a row.
The air was dead and up ahead danced the professor, heel
and toe,
He turns to me and "Mike," says he I'll sleep through this
class I guess;
But if I do I'm hoping you won't refuse my last request."

Well he seemed so low that I couldn't say no; then he says
with a sort of a moan:
"Its the cursed boredom and its got right hold, till I'm asleep
clear through to the bone.
Yet it ain't failing, its my awful dread of a bad night sleep that
pains;
So I want you to promise that foul or fair, you'll watch over
my sleeping remains."

Now a pal's rest is a thing to bless, and I swore I would not
fail;
The class went on and we started to yawn, but God! he looked
ghastly pale.
He was slumped in his seat and began to sleep and dream of
his home in Tenakee;
By break time a sleeping corpse was all that remained of Sam
McGee.

There wasn't a breath in that land of death and I scribble
horror driven,
With a corpse half hid, that I couldn't get rid because of a
promise given;
It was slumped in its seat, but it seemed to say: "You may tax
your brawn and brain,
But you promised true and its up to you, watch over this
peaceful refrain."

Now a promise made is a debt unpaid, although there was no
    consideration.
In the moments to come, though my lips were numb, in my
    heart how I cursed that chump.
Through the long, long night under the florescent lamp light,
    while the students howled out their woes
To the indifferent professor – My God! how I loathed that
    thing!

And every moment that quiet clay, seemed to louder and
    louder snore.
And on I went though my hand was spent, and my ink was
    growing low;
The lecture was bad and the professor mad, but I swore I
    would not give in;
And I would often hum to the dreadful thing, and he would
    harken with a grin!

Till it came to that part of the night when the professor was
    full of spite,
And his gleaming eyes pierced through the light.
He looked at us and he thought a bit, then he spied my
    sleeping chum;
Then "Here," thought I with a sudden cry, "Is his next
    vic-tim!"

Some theorems he tore from a book of lore and mixed them
    with conjecture;
Some briefs he found that were lying around and stirred them
    in the mixture.
The professor roared, and shook the board – such a rage you
    seldom see;
Then he buried a question in that mess of deception and
    hurled it at Sam McGee.

And I took a hike, for I didn't like to hear him suffer so;
And the professor scowled, and the students howled and the
    ventilators began to blow.
It wasn't that hot, but the sweat rolled down my cheeks and I
    think I know why.

The professor spoke and belched fire and smoke that stuck to
    the ceiling on high.

I don't know how long in the hall, I wrestled with grizzly fear;
But the students came out and began to laugh and shout ere
    again I ventured near;
I was sick with dread, but I bravely said:"I'll just take a peak
    inside.
I guess his goose is cooked and it's time I looked"; …then the
    door I opened wide.

There sat Sam, looking cool and calm in the heart of the
    professor's roar;
And he wore a smile you could see a mile and he said, "Please
    close that door.
It's fine in here, but I greatly fear that you will stop this wrath
    of the Lord–
Since I left Tenakee up in the northern sea, it's the first time, I
    ain't been bored!"

> *There are strange things done under the florescent sun,*
>   *By the people who study the law.*
> *The men's john holds its secret yawns*
>   *That would make the ABA's blood run cold.*
> *The students at night have seen queer sights,*
>   *But the strangest they ever did see.*
> *Was the night in Labor law, when the professor saw,*
>   *The slumbering Sam McGee.*

p. Radin

THE TRAIL
1979

I feel as if I walk alone
A banquet hall deserted
Whose lights have fled,
Whose garlands dead,
And all but me departed.

— Winston Churchill

e were off up the Chilkoot Trail – four of us on the path out of the abandoned town of Dyea located at the northern end of the Inside Passage near Skagway, Alaska.

Our timing could not have been better. The trail had been closed for weeks because of flooding and now we were the first on the trail since it had been opened. We could escape the crowds.

It had been a long time since I'd had a 40 pound pack on my back, but I was in shape as were the others. It was 33 miles to where the railroad and the trail crossed on the other side of the divide that separated waters bound for the Bering Sea and those headed of the Gulf of Alaska.

This was the famous Trail of '98 that saw North America's "Last Great Gold Rush." It might well have been called a fool's gold rush because 50,000 people struggled in vain across the passes or up the Yukon River to Dawson only to find all the good ore spots had been staked out a year before they arrived. These people spent $60 million, and only $10 million in gold was taken out of Dawson that first year.

But the stories that these people told of their rush for over-night fortunes filled books for years to come. One of these storytellers was Jack London who left San Francisco ten days after the first ship landed with the news of gold. He was in the second wave of stampeders and made it up to Dawson before the river froze in 1897. The first wave was those already in Alaska and the Yukon when the strike was made. The third wave was the most famous and came over the wintry pass of the Chilkoot and camped and built boats on Lake Bennett, and then floated down to Dawson after the ice went out in 1898.

The Chilkoot Trail in more recent years has become a National Park on both sides of the international border, in part, because nobody used it for anything for 100 years except hikers wanting to re-live the adventure. The importance of the Chilkoot Trail was that it is only 25 miles from navigable water on the Pacific to navigable water on Lake Bennett, which then flowed 2,000 miles through the Yukon and Alaska.

We toiled up the steep trail which, after the first eight miles, gained altitude with every step. The stampeders had floated supplies eight miles up the trial on the river that ran down the canyon, thus reducing the distance they had to go to the top. Each stampeder was required to bring in 2,000 pounds of provisions (one year's supplies) to prevent starvation in Dawson and the Yukon. Much of this food and supplies would later be sold to the earlier arrivals at Dawson who had a claim and needed food. Those who sold the grub upon their arrival at Dawson generally only wanted out at that point — Jack London not the least of them. For many years the trail was abandoned after the railroad went through White Pass and then to Bennett Lake a few years after 1898.

The other trail known as White Pass also leads through a 3,000 foot pass which is several miles west of the Chilkoot Trail. It was also called Dead Horse Pass where over 3,000 horses and mules died carrying their loads to the interior. They died in their tracings from lack of food, exhaustion and cold.

The canyon walls were steep as we hiked along admiring the hanging glaciers on both sides. We camped that night and even found firewood — a delicacy that would not exist on top of the pass.

p. kadir

Fortunately I had brought a bottle of elixir that cooled the atmosphere while we fought over how to cook dinner.

　　The next morning one of our members showed how he could kick a branch that was six feet off the ground. He did it, much to my surprise, but he forgot to stretch beforehand and his knee was to give him problems later.

That day was spent mostly scrambling over boulders the size of small houses. I was amazed at their proportions. Jack London claimed he hauled 150 pound loads over these same rocks. I swore I had 150 pounds on my back though my bath room scale said 40 pounds.

When we reached the Scales, I was impressed. Seldom had I crawled up a 40% pitch on all fours which someone mistakenly called a trail. Had this not been the historic route, I am certain the National Park Service would never allow this trail to exist. While I inched my way up the wall, the high kicking member of that morning scrambled to the top pulled down his pants so a Park Service lady could examine his knee. We all claimed to have knee problems at the top like our companion, but the lady Park Ranger was becoming suspicious.

The remains of a small plane that had been a few feet shy of making the pass was embedded in the rock wall. The wreckage seemed symbolic of all the shattered dreams that rested on this hill. Probably the most famous picture of all is the stampeders standing in a line while mounting the Scale, one step at a time in the winter. On top, the Mounties checked each stampeder to make sure he had his ton of grub.

Immediately on the other side of the pass was snow and a lake full of ice. The wind at the top of this pass is notorious and was blasting misty, cloudy air which made us decide against an extended pause at the top.

We hiked down the mountain to the next wide spot in the trail where we camped with people coming from the other side. This camp had no wood for a fire, because the trees were midgets from the deep snow. Also, the park rangers frowned on burning artifacts for fires.

Continuing on the next day, we arrived and camped at a lake not far from Lindemann lake. At Lindemann lake, Jack London had built his boat which he maneuvered through the rapids to Lake Bennett. Later the third wave would build mainly on Bennett lake because most of the timber was gone above.

We threw ourselves in the lake that night to prove our manhood but found out we were still the same when we came out. We were still fighting over how to cook the food and we were running low on whiskey. I recited Robert Service to the group, but failed to soothe the passions. I had made the mistake of not bringing medicine to treat a skin problem from which I suffered at times, and I was experiencing considerable discomfort. It reminded me of Jack London when he was attacked with scurvy and had to flee from the Yukon to save his life. Though Jack London made millions off his northern tales, he harbored a bitterness toward the land that had so unmercifully attacked his body. I was beginning to feel the same way.

I was not feeling comfortable in this group on this trip and the problem was largely mine. I have read several books on people in the wilderness and the person writing often is portrayed as a well adjusted individual who only seeks harmony in the wilderness. Knowing such a writer, I felt his books put him in synchronization with the wilderness but he personally seemed on the borders of human relations.

As a potential alcoholic and a future Twelve Stepper, I could never be sure if I was running to the wilderness or from something else. What was certain, however, was that I had not cornered the market on knowledge of the world nor of myself.

The next day we strolled into Bennett Lake Station where we planned to catch the train back down to civilization. We found in the ledger along the trail thousands of other signatures of wayfarers who had traveled the same trail. For awhile we thought we were the only ones across since Jack London! We vented our rage by putting a remark next to the name of someone we knew who was a Forest Service naturalist in Juneau. Beside his signature he now proclaimed that this should all be clear cut!

We wolfed down our food at the train station and swapped lies with the other travelers and hikers.

At Lake Bennett was a church made out of discarded, short, unusable pieces of wood that the stampeders built to while away their time until the ice went out. When the ice did go out, the church remained as it is today — uncompleted.

We hopped the train of the narrow gauge railroad and departed Lake Bennett which lies all the more deserted today because the regular train no longer goes that far.

p. kadin

THE BAY
1980

Why Mike, you are getting right with the program.

—Chuck Stotts, an old time Alaskan

I had just taken my first bar exam, and not knowing there would be many more, I felt a great relief. The next day my main squeeze and I flew out of Juneau in Southeast Alaska on a jet plane for Glacier Bay, sixty miles west. Because of the mountains and the short distance to travel, one could look directly out the window and see trees. One could look up and see trees. Not all jet liners offer this service.

We disembarked from the plane at Gustavus, Alaska, and hopped a bus to Glacier Bay National Park campground and lodge. We tented that night in the rain. The next morning we talked with the soggy refugees who had been up the bay for several days and who badly needed a spin and dry. The bay is part of the rain forest stretching a thousand miles up the coast from the State of Washington and here receives up to seventy-five inches of rain a year. The heavy rainfall combined with the high mountain peaks of the Mt. Fairweather range produce the twelve tidewater glaciers of the bay. People not prepared in body, mind and equipment for the damp climate are sometimes humbled by the

p. leadin

experience. Climate controlled foreign cruise ships are popular in the bay for that reason.

These particular refugee/campers lacked proper equipment. The best gear is synthetic pile or wool in a combination with rain gear and/or Gortex, preferably a set of both. A good tent is essential. Down is generally worthless.

My experience has been that after three days of camping in a deluge everything is wet. It doesn't matter how good your equipment or how strong your skills. After that, its' simply how long you can endure feeling like a wet, cold sponge.

We rented a two-person decked canoe which we could not distinguish from a two-person kayak, since neither of us had experience in a kayak or decked canoe. We paddled around a small island for the day, honing our skills to a razor sharp edge. Greater length and less weight per person means more speed in a two-person boat, but it requires paddling in unison and a stable relationship. The outer edge of the island faces the entrance to the bay and beyond is Icy Straits and the Pacific . Here the current splitting on the island and coming together during the changing tides created colliding currents and generated turbulence. It wasn't a safe place.

After a day of paddling, we boarded a boat blooming with tourists to travel up the bay. When the plankton blooms, so do the tourists. The plankton (a small algae) feeds the krill (a small crustacean); the krill feed the whales; and the whales satiate the tourists. The locals feed on the tourists. The food chain works.

The small fifty foot cruise boat transports people into the eastern arm of the bay (Muir Inlet), daily, to view the marine life and the largest collection of tidewater glaciers in the temperate world. Another over night cruise boat explores the other arm, Tarr Inlet.

While traveling up the bay, the sun drove the clouds away, and when we lowered our craft into the water (as well as ourselves), the sky was a massive blue void with a sole radiant star. For three or four weeks during the Southeast Alaskan summer, the wind blows towards the south from the land rather than from the ocean. This northern wind blows the clouds out to sea leaving a carpeted blue heaven above. We had hit the jackpot!

On the cruise boat, the skipper had related how one kayaker had been to Glacier Bay previously and had anticipated the usual rain. Instead he was burnt and fried by the brilliant but unexpected sunshine and made a prisoner in his tent by the sun's rays. When ships came by, he paddled out and begged for sun tan lotion.

As we rowed in unison from the cruise boat, Reid's glacier was bombing the inlet with thousand pound icebergs in the dazzling sun. We kept our distance from the tidewater giant and landed our craft on a spit of land that cut Reid's glacier inlet off from Muir Inlet (the one we had traveled up). Beaching our craft, we pitched our tent above the high tide line. People unfamiliar with twenty foot tides often fall victim, discovering their boat floating off or filled with water. One group paddled a thousand miles from Seattle to Glacier Bay then left their boats under a floating ramp which pinned their kayak, cameras and gear under water when the tide rose. Varying tides are not the only hazard to a kayak. Another group stored food under their boat. A grizzly bear ripped through the boat to get at the grub.

Though our campsite was crushed rock, it was level which is more than Tracy Arm offered (a National Wilderness area in Southeast Alaska featuring tidewater glaciers as the main event). Small icebergs littered our beach like stranded whales deposited and deserted by the tide. They provided ice for our drinks in the evening. In the past, glacier ice was used by fisherman to preserve fish until delivered to market. More recently, an enterprising individual was gathering icebergs in Tracy Arm with a back hoe and barge. A market has developed in Japan for glacier ice in cocktails because the ice lasts longer (made denser by pressure) and as it melts, and expands from its dense dark blue condition, it pops!

Where we camped, plant life was non-existent. Traveling down Muir Inlet is traveling forward in time: the further one travels the younger the vegetation. Two hundred years ago the British explorer, Capt. Vancouver, sailed past the mouth of Glacier Bay and saw a wall of ice. One hundred years later John Muir, the naturalist and explorer, entered the bay by canoe and paddled for fifteen miles. That day we had sailed thirty miles.

Traveling the bay is voyaging by time machine. The further one travels into the bay the less time the land has been exposed and the less time for plant life to grow. At the entrance to the bay, the trees are two hundred years old. Where we camped the land had only been exposed for twenty years and little life had taken hold. Though we were at sea level, the barren rocks made the deserts of the American Southwest seem like a rain forest.

The glaciers of the bay are the key to vegetation and exposed rock. Tidewater glaciers are not like land-lubber glaciers. Glaciers that reach the ocean push a mound of dirt, rock, and debris in front of them. Resting on the bottom of the sea, they use a covering of mud and sediment as insulation to stay cool and frosty, particularly below sea level. With this protective coating of mud, they advance miles into the sea. Eventually, the glacier advances too far and too deep. The seawater seeps past the protective covering and meltdown begins. As the glacier retreats, further covering is lost. As a Glacier Bay naturalist pointed out, the glaciers simply "unzip." In some cases, the regression continues until the glacier climbs out of the sea like a fish in search of evolution. Such was the case with the Grand Pacific Glacier in the western arm of Glacier Bay.

The Grand Pacific Glacier in Tarr Inlet had been retreating for two hundred years like the Muir Glacier. In climbing out of the water, it created the only possibility for a Pacific Canadian port between Seward, British Columbia and the Arctic Ocean. The Canadians planned a road and a port for the Yukon and interior of Northern Canada.

However, by last reports the Grand Pacific Glacier is again advancing into the sea having conveyor belted (by advancing and melting) rock and insulation to its face. Thus, tidewater glaciers remind us of animals who eons ago climbed out of the water to wander the land, then, finding it not to their liking, returned to the sea retaining their air breathing capabilities as marine mammals. Lungs allow marine mammals to have a higher body temperature.

These tidewater glaciers have advanced and retreated many times through the years. During this last retreat, tree stumps were exposed that had grown after the previous retreat and been covered over after the last advance of the ice.

Glaciers on the land act with more regularity. If the earth gets colder, they advance; if warmer, they retreat, generally. A one degree change in the mean average temperature can send glaciers retreating or advancing. Most glaciers on earth are retreating. In comparison to the warm age of the dinosaurs, we are still coming out of the last ice age that came to a close 20,000 years ago. In the early part of this millennium, there was a mini-ice age. That was when Hans Christian and his silver skates slid across the frozen canals of Holland. The canals don't freeze as much today.

The tip of Muir Inlet had but a couple of tenants in residence that day: us. The other spectators had been rained out and the stadium belonged to us, but the show went on. We paddled up the inlet after making camp, searching for Muir Glacier. The pack ice was thick from the collapsing glacier we sought which had retreated around the corner of a mountain. We were forced to skim over ice flows with our rigid kayak. Eventually, we quit paddling because we feared being trapped by the pack ice if the wind shifted. We tried to climb over the mountain that hid the glacier. At one point, it was necessary to cross an ice bridge in order to ford a stream. The area had been covered with snow and ice and what remained was an ice bridge preserved by pebbles and debris in the ice that insulated it from the sun and rain.

We turned chicken and retreated, because the possible reward was not equal to the danger. John Muir, the great naturalist and explorer, would have strolled across as if on a Sunday walk. His adventures while discovering and exploring Glacier Bay one hundred years ago are accounts of America's best "light" explorer. With barely the clothes on his back and hardtack (a type of beef jerky with added fat), he spent days on the glaciers without a fire. At night he slept on the ice, soaked by the rain with only a blanket.

We headed down the mountain to our kayak. On the icebergs the seals bathed in the sun. The sea is murky from the crushed and suspended rock "flour" created by the glaciers. Nutrients are plentiful in Southeast Alaskan waters because the water temperatures are more uniform than in warmer climates, allowing nutrients to be brought up from the bottom. This is particularly true in the bay where glacial rivers under the ice increase the nutrients coming up to form the basis of life. Southeast Alaska and Glacier Bay are a warehouse of food. With the long summer daylight, plankton at the bottom of the food chain grow profusely in summer making the water a dark rich green. In Glacier Bay, the water looked cloudy and milky from the lighter glacial water that sits on top of the heavier, clearer salt water.

We re-floated our kayak and headed back. While kayaking in thirty-four degree water may seem risky, it is no more dangerous than hurtling down a crowded freeway at 60 m.p.h. surrounded by two thousand pounds of glass and metal: just don't screw up. Mistakes can be fatal!

We dined that night on freeze dried food and enjoyed the great solitude and awe inspiring peaks in the twilight hours that lasted past midnight. Down the inlet, a black bear was dining on a camper. Risk-free adventure is a contradiction in terms. Still, I felt safer than on any road in America.

The next day the good news of sunshine had leaked out and floatplanes landed like seagulls disgorging campers and kayaks. Dome tents sprang up like mushrooms on that barren land below us, proving that something could grow there.

Most people visit the bay in large foreign cruise ships. Large domestic cruise liners can't compete with the minuscule wages paid foreign sailors and the lax safety regulations of foreign registered vessels. Thus, when new slots come open for cruise ships to enter Glacier Bay, the summer home of the Humpback whale, the foreign cruise lines gorge themselves on American tourists in an American National Park while domestic sailors and ships starve. In America's National Park only foreigners operate large cruise ships.

Though we know why tourists exist in the bay nobody has yet explained why the earth fluctuates in and out of ice ages. There are many theories concerning the fluctuation between the earth's tropical climate during the dinosaur era and the subsequent numerous ice ages. Ideas range from a self-regulating polar ice cap that melts and re-freezes because of currents that flow to it for a time and then are blocked; to the rising of the Himalayas and the Rocky Mountains which may have effected the climate enough to cause fluctuations; to variating cycles in the earth's rotation around the sun.

What is obvious, however, is that many things effect the climate of the earth including plants and animals. Human beings have the center stage at this time. Some people argue today that with the gases and fumes we put into the atmosphere, we are creating a green house effect and warming our planet. Maybe we are getting the earth ready for a second coming of the dinosaurs?

When John Muir came to study the mysteries of Glacier Bay a hundred years ago, he had to deal with other puzzles as well. He was visited by one of the first tourist vessels to the bay. However, when the tourists disembarked from their boat, instead of being in awe of the surrounding glaciers, they were far more intrigued by the humble shack Muir had constructed to live in. John Muir could not contain his anger when he saw their attention diverted from the sublime glaciers to his temporary shanty town!

The next day, the small American cruise boat retrieved us and took us back to the more complicated world. The tourists seemed not to have changed as greatly as the bay. Many of them seemed more concerned with our minor attempts to navigate and dock a decked canoe than the sublime glaciers that crowned the landscape.

p.Radin

SEPTEMBER ON THE YUKON
1980

Purpose shall be the firmer,
Heart the keener,
Courage shall be the more,
As our might lessens.

— from *The Battle of Maladin*

At noon it was 30 degrees Fahrenheit. We paddled our canoe through yellow valleys of September leaves. In the Yukon, fall lasts two weeks, as does the Spring. In northern Canada, only a hundred miles from the Arctic Circle, nature has little time to waste. In a week the leaves turn from green to yellow; in another week they are blown from the trees.

We hated that wind. Since the second week out it had blown in our faces for two hundred miles. It blew from the north and brought the Arctic chill. The creeks on the side of the river had frozen. There was ice floating in small pools of slush in the murky, glacial melt river. As soon as the glaciers in the coastal range stopped melting, the river would run clear for a few weeks before it froze over.

Sue was the first to feel the bite of the cold. It had rained during the day and the freezing wind cut through her wool gloves. We made her wind proof gloves out of scraps of plastic patches that we had. She sewed me a pair of wool gloves out of a blanket that we found in a cabin. We also sewed boots out of blankets with dental floss. We felt like Napoleon's army in its retreat from Moscow.

We had put on the Yukon River at Whitehorse, capital of the Yukon Territory, almost two weeks before. It had snowed a foot of snow two days before we left but had then melted. Therefore, anybody who had any brains was off the river. Only a few hunters in power boats ventured out at this time of year — them and ourselves.

The bugs were gone — that was the good part — that and no people. We floated down from Whitehorse on the Yukon River the first day to Lake LaBarge where Sam McGee was famously cremated in Robert Service's poem. It took two days to paddle across that 30 miles of lake.

The Yukon River was at one time the main artery of transportation to the interior. With its navigable waters in the coastal range only 25 miles from the Gulf of Alaska, the prospectors came over the trail of '98 from Skagway, Alaska, and floated 700 miles down to the Klondike River to found Dawson City, the site of North America's Last Great Gold Rush. From its mouth, 2,000 miles away in the Bering Sea, sternwheelers plied the Yukon River bringing goods and people to the interior. The great artery of the Yukon was virtually abandoned in the 1950s when the road went in linking Dawson City to the Alaska-Canadian highway at Whitehorse. Whole towns were evacuated as the trade moved off the river to the road. Today, those abandoned towns, such as Fort Selkirk and Forty Mile, and the deserted Mounty Stations, wood cutter's station, etc. are a living museum of the Yukon's great past. On this river, Jack London ran his boat through Miles Rapids above present day Whitehorse on his way to the Klondike in the year of '97.

It was, now, our second week on the Yukon. The first week had been plenty of sunshine with warm days and fast moving current except for Lake LaBarge. At the town of Carmacks, the road crosses the river and is the halfway point between Whitehorse and Dawson City for both the river and the road. We had come 250 miles in a week and though we had some difficulties, we felt good enough to go another week—220 miles to Dawson City.

From the first day on the second leg of the trip, the wind blew. It only blew in one direction—up river. We had to keep the nose of the canoe in the wind to keep from being turned around and blown up stream. Canoes have little drag in the water, but plenty of sail (the sides of the canoe) to catch wind. Blowing from the north, the wind brought a bitter chill. We had forgotten our heavy winter gloves and boots. For some reason we never considered them.

We rode the waves at Five Finger Rapids where the sternwheelers were winched through and camped on the point of an island. It was one of our worst camps on the trip, nestled in bushes and thorns.

The next morning when I walked around the point from where we had landed, my heart froze when I saw a sweeper. It was a tree, fallen from the shore, laying on top of the water and sweeping it with its branches. Had we come around the island on to that tree we would have been swamped, loosing most of our gear if not our lives. Better canoers than we had died on such things. I was shaken by this brush with oblivion.

Each day we went through our routine — two hours to get on the river; eight hours of paddling with two hours to rest, eat lunch, and explore; two hours to setup camp, build a fire and eat dinner— a 14 hour day from 7 A.M. to 9 P.M.

I was the first one to break under the strain of the cold, the wind, and the thoughts of not making it. Every night I sat at the fire drinking my scotch and getting half drunk. I drank more for fear than pleasure. I knew that if I was hurt we might not get out. Sue, at only 110 pounds, was not big enough to battle the wind and current without help. In the end, I had to get us out and I felt the responsibility.

We carried a shotgun with bear slugs. We saw many grizzly and black bears along the river, but none raided our camps. Moose swam the river at times while we floated by and our fear of them was recorded in how small they appeared in the pictures (because of the

p. Radin

67

great distance we kept from them) even though we used a three power telephoto lens.

Eventually it became too cold to paddle for long stretches and we had to stop and build fires to warm ourselves and to heat rocks that we put in the boat to keep our feet warm.

We were now within a hundred miles of Dawson or three days float. But I wanted out. As we got closer to Dawson we started to see more civilization. We stopped at a homestead to inquire about radioing a helicopter to fly us out. But the expense was too high for Sue. I admired her for that.

After we left the house, the wind blew so hard that it turned our canoe around and being too exhausted and cold to paddle we sat in the river without moving. A power boat passed us going to the homestead we had just left. We felt ridiculous.

There was one time on this trip that I felt as desperate as I did now. Four days out of Whitehorse, I caught a cold and when I laid myself down that night I swore I would not rise the next day, but would tell Sue to get out by herself if she could (the current was stronger with little wind at that point). I have a terrible time with colds. Strangely, I woke the next day and was well — amazing what the body does when it has no other choice. Then Sue became sick.

But I was more desperate now and I wanted off the river. Sue and I had it out in a deserted trapper's cabin 90 miles from Dawson City. I told her we would get out anyway we could even if we had to fly. She agreed this time. But she was probably braver than I.

The next day we stopped at Stewart Island which had a small store and cabins for rent. We were able to arrange transportation out with the owners. They would take us and our canoe to Dawson on their large power boat three days from then. Sue and I were both relieved.

It was a good place to stay over for a few days. If any place could lay claim to Jack London's literary birthplace, it might be Stewart Island. This is where London wintered over for six months during the winter of 1897-98 because of starvation in Dawson City, 80 miles down river.

Here at the intersection of the Stewart and Yukon Rivers, miles from any town, London had listened to the tales of the Yukon and Alaska pioneers who had criss-crossed the land in search of gold for decades. It was those stories and his own adventures that he later wrote about that brought him his first recognition as a writer and earned him his greatest fame.

In the break-up of the Spring of '98 Jack London floated to Dawson City, did a little gold mining and then rafted down the Yukon to the Bering Sea where he worked his way home on a steamer. He had only spent a year in the Northland — never to return. He wondered himself, years later after writing fifty-one volumes on various subjects, why the Yukon and Alaska had so fascinated his readers as compared to his other writings and the rest of his incredible adventures.

It felt good to be at Stewart Island, the little known claimant to the birthplace of Jack London's literary career. After three days in a rented cabin on the island, we rode down river with the present day owners of the place. The eighty miles in a power boat took four hours. The plane flight from Dawson to Whitehorse from which we could view the river took but two hours.

It was a good trip with plenty of adventure, but I felt some resentment that Sue had proven stronger than I.

Try the Yukon River in the summer — a much more pleasant experience (but more bugs and people).

THE ENGINE ROOM
1981

Between my time as a waiter on the ferries and as a purser, I disappeared into the engine room for several years. During this same period, I was studying for the bar exam. One day I emerged from the oil pan (the sump) of a 16 cylinder engine which was the size of a semi-truck that I had been cleaning out by hand, sixty hours a week, for two weeks. As I oozed up from the extremities, completely slimed with oil, another worker in the engine room with a philosophical twist about him said, "This should be good incentive for passing the bar exam."

Ode to A Wiper
adapted from *Invictus* by Ernest Henley

Out of the slime that covers me
Black as the sump from hole to hole
I thank whatever engineers may be
For my filthy soul.

In the fell clutch of the sump,
I've not wince nor cried aloud

In the maze of the bilge,
My head is oily, but unbowed.

Beyond this place of sumps and pumps,
Lies but the horror of the boiler,
And yet the engineers of the ship,
Find me all the bolder.

It matters not how black the stack,
Nor charged with grime the pump.
I am the Master of the bilge
I am the Captain of the sump.

Square rigger —by Rod Dixon

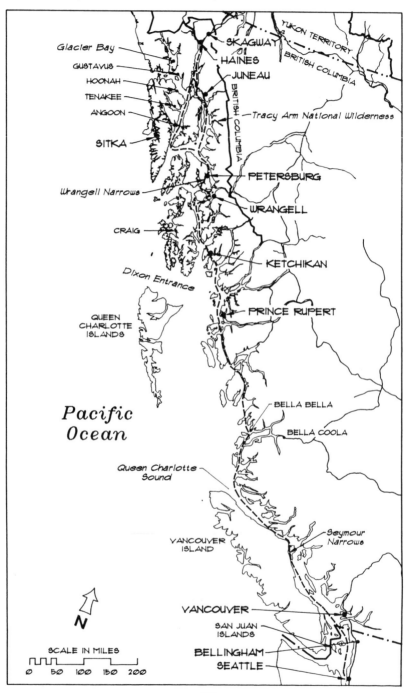

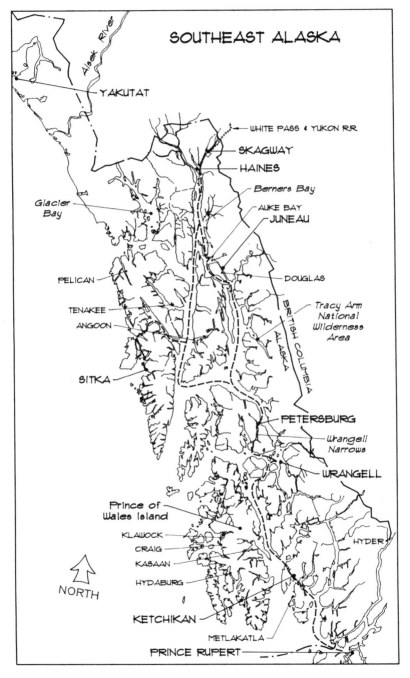

SOUTHEAST ALASKA

ALASKA BOUND

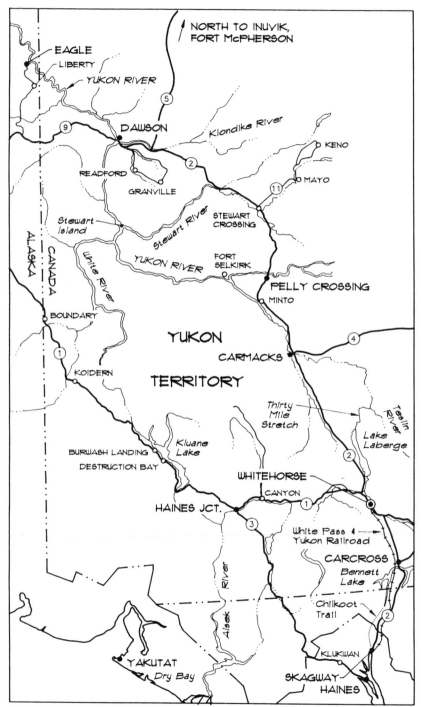

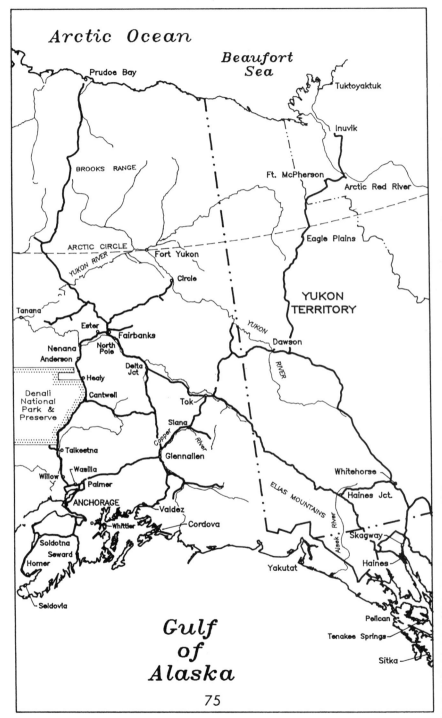

Arctic Ocean

Beaufort Sea

Prudoe Bay

Tuktoyaktuk

Inuvik

BROOKS RANGE

Ft. McPherson

Arctic Red River

Eagle Plains

ARCTIC CIRCLE

YUKON RIVER

Fort Yukon

Circle

YUKON TERRITORY

Tanana

Ester

Fairbanks

YUKON

Nenana
Anderson

North Pole

Dawson

RIVER

Delta Jct.

Healy

Cantwell

Tok

Denali National Park & Preserve

Slana

Copper

River

Talkeetna

Glennallen

Wasilla

Willow

Palmer

ANCHORAGE

Whitehorse

Valdez

ELIAS MOUNTAINS

Haines Jct.

Whittier

Cordova

Soldotna

Skagway

Seward

Alsek River

Homer

Yakutat

Haines

Seldovia

Pelican

Gulf
of
Alaska

Tenakee Springs

Sitka

75

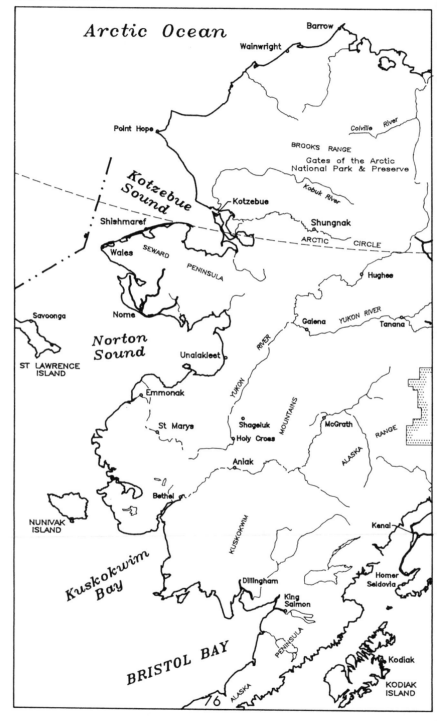

p.Radin

THE ALSEK-MOUNT BLACKADAR EXPEDITION

1983

We few, we happy few, we band of brothers;
For he to-day that sheds his blood with me
Shall be my brother; be he ne'ver so vile
This day shall gentle his condition;
And gentlemen in England, now a-bed
Shall think themselves accurs'd they were not here,
And hold their manhoods cheap whiles any speaks
That fought with us upon Saint Crispin's day.

Henry V — Shakespeare

As I climbed in the helicopter and headed out to find my companions some place on the Alsek River, I could swear the person on the ground who assisted in our departure was smiling and I knew what he was saying to himself, "You think you are going to float Turnback Canyon of the Alsek River? You may as well try to ski down Everest!" Well, he was not going to find me in Turnback Canyon rolled up in a kayak!

I found the other members of the Alsek-Mt. Blackadar Expedition resting on a sandbar in the Alsek, eating lunch and wondering if I would show up. The group had left two days earlier, and had run into bad winds, sluggish currents, and a lot of hard work hauling the two rafts (eight and six man) and two white water kayaks through the water and mud.

The leader of the group and one of the kayakers was Ron Watters who directs the Idaho State University Outdoor Program and has authored several books on river running and winter camping. Cathy Daily was a reporter and co-anchor/newscaster from Pocatello, Idaho. The expedition's scientist, head photographer, and the main man on the oars in No. Two raft was Jim Brock, a professional river guide, Ph.D. candidate (biology), and alpinist. Bob Blackadar rowed raft No. 1 and was the inspiration for the trip as he carried an ice ax with the family coat of arms that he hoped to place on top of Mt. Blackadar, named after his father Walt Blackadar, the first man to run Turnback Canyon. Jerry Dixon was the other crazy or kayaker (the terms are synonymous) besides Ron Watters. Jerry was a biologist in the Yukon-Charlie National Park, an Alaskan homesteader, log cabin builder, smoke-jumper, environmentalist, expert kayaker, humorist, and one of the finest people I have ever met. He is also my brother. D'arcy Dixon (our sister) was a dance instructor at the University of Utah and led all dance exercises on the sandbars along the Alsek. She was especially remembered for her Swan Lake performance at the entrance of Turnback Canyon. I assisted in rowing raft number two.

Six people had converged on the put-in point at Haines Junction from three different directions by plane, car, truck, and finally myself in a chopper: an amazing bit of logistics. From the put-in spot 75 miles west of Whitehorse, Yukon Territory, they had floated down the Dezadeash River to its confluence with the Kaskawulsh River which together formed the Alsek River that flowed 200 miles through Kluane National Park, British Columbia, to Dry Bay, Alaska, and the Pacific Ocean.

The Alsek River was a seldom floated river because half way down is a legendary place called Turnback Canyon. It received its name because it turned back the gold stampeders of 1898 who were headed for the interior. It is a ten mile chute which was formed by the frequent advance of Tweedsmuir glacier pushing the river into the side of Mt. Blackadar. For want of a place to go the river dug a narrow, tortured chasm along the side of the mountain. Turnback Canyon aside, the Alsek River is a difficult river with Class IV rapids and bone-chilling water of 34 degrees Fahrenheit. But Turnback Canyon has become to some kayakers what K2 is to the climbing world: if it is not the toughest runable river, it is a close second. By 1983, only four people had successfully kayaked Turnback Canyon. During a more recent attempt to kayak the canyon, a French Expedition lost a person in the first mile and the rest abandoned their kayaks and were flown out. One person has kayaked Turnback twice. But the man who did it first and the man who did it alone was the legendary Walt Blackadar.

Walt was a physician in Salmon, Idaho, on the banks of the Salmon River and learned to kayak there and later taught Ron Watters to kayak. Walt, unable to get anyone to go with him down the Alsek, decided to do the canyon alone. He left a message with the pilot who dropped him off that if he did not find him at the agreed pick up point to spend $1,000 looking for him and then report him as missing and presumed dead. Walt's story of the first man through Turnback was published in Sports Illustrated and brought him to prominence in the kayaking world. In 1978 Walt Blackadar drowned in a kayaking accident in Idaho. A Canadian friend of his, Klaus Streckmann, had Mt. Blackadar named after him (no small achievement since Walt Blackadar was a foreigner in Canada).

We continued down the glacial waters of the Alsek, the third day on the river for the group and my first. The water of the Alsek being a glacial stream was gray from "rock flour" suspended in the water coming from the glaciers upstream which had ground the rock to a fine powder. It was impossible to see a foot deep in the water and the raft hissed as it slid through the current of liquid rock. Rapids were not called "white water;" they were instead called "gray water" by our group.

That day we spent straining on the oars to make headway on the river and through the "braids", as various arms of the river were called, as they criss-crossed on each other.

We were now in Kluane National Park which meant guns were prohibited, but you could still fight the bears with your knife and stones. Bob Blackadar showed a talent for hunting out bear trails and camping on them.

The air was crisp that day and our feet cold even though we were clothed in ⅛" wet suits. It was also dusty as dried glacial silt from the river was picked up and carried by the wind which built huge Sand dunes along the river and at times blinded us in a dust storm.

The Alsek River was never above 35 degrees Fahrenheit. We were at 3,000 feet, the tree line stopped at 4,000 feet, and the tundra at 5,000 feet. Above that was stone and ice because of our being so far north. The mountain peaks along the river ranged from 5,000 feet up to 14,000 feet within our view and somewhere back beyond our sight was Mt. St. Elias at over 18,000 feet.

There is something mystical about floating through country where there is no sign nor sound nor smell of man other than yourself. There is something almost holy in knowing that many of the mountains seen have no name; that the rapids you will run are not on a map and also have no name; that few people have seen what you now witness. You become almost indignant if you see another footprint or another camp site. You feel as if you have been invited to a command performance of nature with you as the sole audience. You feel enthralled and humble. Possibly you feel that for all man's efforts over millions of years he has yet to conquer this place and that even if man does not endure nature will.

We camped that night at the start of Lowell Lake with Lowell glacier in view. In the morning we crossed the lake created by Lowell glacier receding and floated in amongst the icebergs as large as buildings and cobalt blue. When an iceberg calves off a glacier, it is first deep blue but slowly turns white as the air enters it. Icebergs can be extremely dangerous as the bottoms in the water tend to melt faster than the top in the air and then they flip (water is fifteen times denser than air and melts ice faster even though it has a cooler temperature). Jerry, in his kayak, floated underneath an overhanging arm of an iceberg and after he paddled away the piece of ice crashed into the water — very educational.

After Lowell Lake we hit Discretion Rapids (our name) which the rafts discretionally avoided through a side channel of the river. The kayakers had some practice. Class IV (on a scale from one to six), they said, just below Lava Falls of the Grand Canyon (big water by anybody's terms, but nothing like Turnback which is a solid Class VI). Ron slalomed the waves while Jerry went right through them.

With the kayakers riding point as the scouts to see what was ahead, the rafters followed with the supplies and camping gear. This was necessary since there was no map of the river except for large geographical maps and no one knew for certain what the river held for us.

The next rapids we named Delightful since we all ran it without incident. Look out for the hole on the upper half; Jim Brock did a beautiful oar sweep which saved us from a certain drenching if not a complete flip. One thing about Bob Blackadar; he sized up a rapid in a matter of minutes, whether to run or not, and never changed his mind. Probably much like his father.

We camped that night on our traditional bear trail (we saw six bears that trip). Bob would have his tent set up before the rest of us got out of the boats. Jim Brock was a tireless workhorse rowing the raft, taking experiments (river ecology), taking pictures, and then baking cakes half the night.

The next day we floated down the river with Mt. Blackadar (as we were to later find out) looming in front of us with its thousands of feet of hanging glaciers. We camped that night at the foot of Mt. Blackadar and planned our assault the next day to make Bob the first man on top.

The first 1,000 feet (of the 5,000 foot climb) was pure brush — a veritable jungle. The next 2,000 feet was beautiful tundra and mountain flowers. At this point D'arcy and Cathy turned back down the

mountain (as we lacked the necessary equipment for them), and the five of us went on across the snow fields. Ron was on point and Jim brought up the rear as the two most experienced alpinists. The snow was soft enough that we did not need crampons, but the ice axes and finally ropes became a must. We followed the ridge to the top — the only route possible for us. While roped together, we experienced winds of 40 to 50 m.p.h.. On the ridge I stared down into space of several thousand feet on either side of me and was vaguely reminded of jumping out of an airplane in my youthful past. Both experiences seemed absurd and caused almost detached reflection on just what made people do certain things. For me, it was boredom. For the others, I am sure they had their reasons.

The last 200 feet Ron rigged a stationary line which we clamped into and headed for the top. We all watched as Bob Blackadar put the first footprints on the summit of Mt. Blackadar and planted an ice ax with his family name and coat of arms on it with an engraving of Walt Blackadar in a kayak.

The way down was easier and much more fun as we slid down the snow fields. I noticed how the cliffs did not look as menacing as before. Ron said one gets used to it. He also said it was 5.4 in difficulty (on a scale of one to six). The number system between kayaking and climbing is not directly corresponding — the average participant may be Class III in kayaking and class 5.5 in climbing. 5.4 was enough for me.

The last 1,000 feet of descent was one of the most ignominious retreats from a mountain I ever hope to experience, as we stumbled and fell head-over-heels through a jungle of brush and devil's club (a long branch full of thorns). We thought we had found a quick way down the mountain and instead fell down a cliff of thorns.

That night we all were in rare form. Jerry continued to humor us with his ads for Grey Poupon mustard, arguing that it was the backbone of all major expeditions. Jim Brock continued with his experiments (that night it was water samples) and his cooking. Bob Blackadar read the foreword of Ron's White water River Book which was dedicated to Walt Blackadar. We all toasted Walt, the mountain, Turnback Canyon, and each other. Then as usual the talk turned to old war stories of past deeds, rivers floated, how big were the rapids covered by Lake Powell in Cataract Canyon of the Colorado? How good was Walt Blackadar? And how good was Rob Lessor (the only man to do Turnback Canyon twice)? Was the Grand Canyon of the

Stikine (also in Canada) the Everest of white water river running? What about the new rivers being run in Nepal and Tibet? Slowly one by one we went off to bed, D'arcy singing to us as we fell asleep. Seldom had I felt such contentment.

The next day was rest day before we hit Turnback Canyon. Every morning Bob Blackadar would get up and say, "It doesn't get any better than this." He probably was right. Never could you find a nicer group of people nor a more beautiful land. We rested that day. Some people hiked, some wrote, some did experiments, and some bathed in the river (putting my head under the icy water for 30 seconds affected my equilibrium so that I could not stand up). I guessed a person in the water at 34 degrees Fahrenheit would lose feeling in his limbs in five minutes, consciousness in another five minutes, and his life in the next five minutes. The Frenchman who died during the French Expedition of Turnback Canyon had been dragged under by the current with his kayak and had floated underwater beneath his companions and was finally discovered miles down the murderous canyon.

The next day we floated to Turnback Canyon and saw the glacier ten miles wide that fronted and created Turnback Canyon by pushing up against Mt. Blackadar. Just before the canyon we stopped and waited for the helicopter which was to lift the rafts and gear around the canyon. Here we also visited a cairn (a small memorial) in memory of Walt Blackadar, put there by his friends.

The helicopter came and took off with the first load across the ice. Jerry and Ron went with this load and were to take a look at the canyon on the way back to see if it was runnable. The pilot (an amiable person who insisted he had never flown a helicopter before) said the water was high. After half an hour the helicopter returned and Jerry and Ron got out; their faces were grim. To them the canyon was "skull and cross-bones." The water was high and made the canyon even more deadly than it was normally. This was not to be their time to tempt the fates and to dance with death. If their time would come, it was not to be this trip. The number of kayakers to conquer the canyon was to remain at four and the number that died in the canyon was to remain at one.

I went with the final load across the ice. I waved good-bye to my friends at the other end of Turnback Canyon as we dropped the last load. Five people would float on for another week to the Gulf of Alaska and Dry Bay and then fly to Juneau (unfortunately these last days were spent in almost constant rain as they neared the sea and D'arcy was heard to say, "We are breaking the fun meter this time.") My brother, Jerry, and I had to return to our jobs.

On the way back the pilot dipped down to give me a look at Turnback Canyon. It looked like death to me: ten miles of a narrow, twisted, snaking chute. It bore no resemblance to the rest of the river. Even the rock looked different. There were "Double Indemnity" and "Percolator." There were the "S turns" where the Frenchman had died. It was hard to see exactly how big the waves were because the water was all gray, but it looked like trying to kayak in a washing machine. I was glad my brother Jerry had decided to pass on this one. Some days you go for it and some days you walk away.

Jerry and I flew up the river in the 'copter and saw several bears in the valley of the Alsek as well as some beautiful ice falls at Lowell glacier. In Haines Junction (where we had left our cars), we talked with the pilot and listened to his story of how they had tried with helicopter assistance to save the Frenchman who had died in Turnback Canyon. Finally, after I said farewell to my brother, I climbed into my car and headed down the highway to Haines where I caught a ferry to Juneau, Alaska. It had been a great journey in a mystical place with the best of friends and family. But in the back of my mind I had to wonder about those people like Walt Blackadar, Rob Lessor and others who bite off that extra bit of life that I could never taste.

p. Radin

THE GREAT ALONE
1985

Were you ever out in the Great Alone, when the moon was
    awful clear,
And the icy mountains hemmed you in with a silence you
    most could hear;
With only the howl of the timber wolf, and you camped out
    there in the cold,
A half dead thing in a stark, dead world, clean mad for that
    muck called gold;
While high overhead, green, yellow and red, The northern
    lights swept in bars? —
Then you have an idea that the music meant... hunger and
    night and the stars.

from *The Shooting of Dan McGrew* — Robert Service

Thirteen dogs strain at their harnesses. They howl and yelp and jump forward with their full weight to jerk the sled into motion. I am sitting on the sled, bundled in down, capped in beaver skin and encased in Arctic gloves that come up to my elbows.

Greg makes last minute adjustments before our departure from Shungnak, Alaska, on a trip down the frozen Kobuk River and up to the pass that leads to Gates of the Arctic National Park. A metal hook on a leather strap buried in the snow keeps the sled motionless. Sled dogs that spend most of their lives chained to a post become adrenaline junkies in the harness. Yelling at them does no good and Greg doesn't try. He just holds on to the sled with one hand while standing on the snow anchor as he finishes tying down gear and donning his huge sled mittens. The long, heavily insulated gloves are attached by a string running across the shoulders that allow him to take off his mittens without losing them and put them back on quickly. At 10 degrees below zero Fahrenheit, exposed flesh freezes rapidly.

Greg is a school teacher at the Eskimo village of Shungnak, Alaska, located above the Arctic Circle, south of the Brooks Range, and 400 miles from Russia. We are heading out on a crystal blue day to meet my brother and his wife, at the pass leading to the Park. They also teach at Shungnak and left earlier with their dog team.

Pulling the snow anchor out and giving a shout, we are off! The dogs pull as if the Great Satan himself is after them. The chilled air "through the parka's fold, stabs like the driven nail"[1] at 20 MPH. Before us spreads the white Arctic plain slowly rolling away. The lead dog steers the way with a "haw" (left) or "gee" (right) from the driver (there are no reins to guide as with horses).

Through the blue void above shines the bright but heatless Arctic sun. Spring is the time for dogsledding: it is still too cold to melt the winter's accumulated snow, but there is light until 9 P.M. Shungnak gains five minutes of sunlight a day until June 21st when the sun never sets. Sunglasses are a must as the sun reflects off the great whiteness, burning and blinding the eyes.

We rendezvous with Jerry, my brother, and Deborah, his wife, at the pass leading to Gates of the Arctic National Park. Because it is the least accessible National Park in the nation, there are times when the one person who runs the park exceeds the number of visitors. It is good to know one National Park has no freeways to it and that we might be the only animals on two feet.

Having dropped me off, Greg heads back to town with his team. Jerry and Deborah's team is smaller — seven dogs. Deborah runs the team while Jerry and I tie dogs to our waists to tow us on our cross-country skis. We both carry 40-pound packs, but energy is largely spent staying vertical while being yanked and pulled by exuberant huskies. The remaining gear is carried on the sled.

Bear with wolves, Artist unknown

We ski and mush to the top of the pass. A road runs up from the Kobuk River to an undeveloped world-class copper mine in the canyon. It remains under-exploited because there is no road to the sea (200 miles away). Only a few buildings and one mine shaft testify to mankind's endeavors here.

We camp at the top of the pass. The dogs are put on a chain (through which they cannot chew). We build a fire and cook their food. They wolf it down. I am hoping to hear wolves on this trip, but the dogs' keen hearing picks up the wolves' howl first and then the huskies start howling and nothing else can be heard. Wolves make dogs nervous because they eat huskies right off their chains.

Jerry has a large beard that is often covered by ice caused by his breath crystallizing. Deborah, his wife, is a blonde beauty from Vermont whom Jerry met in Shungnak. She drives a team as well as Jerry. Alaska is the place where men are men and the women win the Iditarod (a 1,200 mile dogsled race won by women five times in six years).

It's 20 degrees below zero Fahrenheit at night around the campfire, but that's comfortable. We tear at caribou meat cooked over a wood fire. The last time Jerry and Deborah were on the trail it was 40 below and too cold to comfortably eat with exposed hands. They jumped up and down in front of a roaring fire to stay warm. They talk calmly about it, considering there are experienced trappers who swear going out at 40 below is mushing with death as your lead dog.

Sitting around the campfire enjoying a little "hooch" and a cigar after dinner reminds Jerry and me of our first winter camp out, in Utah, 15 years ago. We spent most of our time cooking frozen deer meat over a portable gas stove (a slow process -- we did not know to spike the meat on a stick and shove it in the fire). We were in our twenties then. Tonight we are in our thirties, eating caribou meat in the Brooks Range, with a dog team.

As kids in our early teens, we watched the TV series "The Alaskans" and threw around pokes of gold pretending we were sourdoughs and prospectors. Since that time we had both headed north in pursuit of dreams: I built a log house in Southeast, Alaska where I worked on cruise ships and drifted in and out of law school and bar exams; Jerry for a period had his log cabin in historic Eagle, Alaska, on the banks of the mighty Yukon river, while smoke-jumping forest fires and re-writing his Master's thesis in biology.

Jerry had called me north from my homestead 2,000 miles away, saying we had to mush dogs together through the Great Alone. I could not resist. We have come full circle. We are living the dreams of our youth and feeling strangely successful.

Sleeping in tents, we prepare a bottle of hot water to warm our feet and for liquid in the morning. We also sleep with our ski boots so they will not be as hard as bricks tomorrow.

The next day we push through the pass and past the under-developed copper mine. The mountains loom on both sides of us. Few glaciers exist in the Brooks Range—not enough precipitation. It is actually considered a desert. Huge sand dunes line the Kobuk River.

In the pass during a brief stop, the dogs pull out the snow anchor and head down hill with the sled, dragging the driver behind. Deborah hangs on to save the sled and gear from destruction or loss. Jerry races after her while I hold his dog. At the bottom of the hill, the sled stops. Deborah has held on. Tough lady. Many mushers have died when their team departed for home with all their provisions, leaving them behind.

For centuries, dogs had been the chosen means of Arctic transportation and exploration. Perspiring through their tongues, they have no problem with moisture build-up on their skin or fur as do humans or other draft animals. They carry their tent and sleeping bag with them — their tail for their nose and their fur coat. A frozen fish or two a day is their only need. If times are tough, then they become fuel for each other and for humans. Explorers Amundsen and Peary used them in their conquests of the poles. Scott did not and he paid for his mistake of using horses with his life. In more recent times, snowmobiles, being less expensive and easier to handle, have had greater popularity than dogs.

Sled dogs (even if for recreation) are considered work animals and not pets. If they do not pull long and hard, they generally develop what some people in Alaska refer to as a fatal case of "bullet-itis".

We enter the Gates of the Arctic National Park and ski down a river and make camp. Multi-thousand foot peaks reach for the clear blue heavens on all sides. There are caribou tracks but not their makers. We feel safe. We have come home. For us, safety and home is knowing there is nothing over the next hill but wilderness. That is true security. For all the beauty of Europe (where we brothers both lived and often return), human hands mark the far side of every hill. That is not security.

We camp and it's not as cold as the last camp but it's crowded with many small trees and brush. Jerry and Deborah meticulously feed their dogs cooked fish and warmed dog food. On the trail dogs are always fed before humans.

I am tired tonight. I crawl into my nylon dome tent early, where I am enshrouded in an outer sleeping bag shell, nestled in a down bag, layered on an inflated mat, cocooned in a vapor barrier (keeping the bag dry and me warm and clammy), smothered in polypropylene clothing, feet buried in down booties, and my head topped with a beaver skin hat. My prayer tonight is to prevent a call to nature. If you have a problem getting up in the morning, try it at 20 below! (Jerry says he brought the dog team mainly to pull me out of bed.)

The next day we spend the normal four hours to eat and break camp (it takes four hours to make camp as well). Then we head back to Shungnak. While traveling on a frozen river, Deborah and the sled break through the ice. My heart climbs up into my throat and refuses to leave. But the dogs keep pulling and soon they are out of the water which appears only a foot deep. Jerry explains that rivers often overflow their covering sheet of ice when a crack opens. I hope my pounding heart does not show through my clothing.

Heading back before the pass, the temperature rises to almost 20 degrees above, but a fierce wind tears at us. The dogs refuse to move in the wind. Deborah is exhausted. I go ahead and drag the lead dog while Jerry takes the sled. Afterwards Jerry and I say that it was the best part of the trip. "That was just like on the first ascent of Mt. Blackadar when that 50 m.p.h. wind tried to blow us off the top," he says. Now even Deborah thinks we are crazy.

We build an igloo tonight at our old campsite which Jerry and Deborah will use through the Spring. The snow is not hard enough for making good snow blocks but we weld them together with slush made from water and snow. At 10 above water still freezes quickly. Branches support the roof. I sleep in it tonight to test it out. It works well; but if it caves in, 400 pounds of ice will be my tombstone.

The next day we mush back to Shungnak. In the distance we see Old Man Mountain (south of Shungnak and the Brooks Range) which Jerry climbed a few weeks back. He and a friend built a snow cave half way up to spend the night. The mountain appears small compared to the Brooks Range, one of the last great unexploited areas on earth. Having worked in an open pit copper mine in Utah, I know what man does to the land. Some day much of what we have seen will be gone under man's tread.

At the eastern end of the Brooks Range on the borders of Canada and the Arctic sea, bugle calls are coming from afar. The battle lines are being drawn over the Arctic National Wildlife Refuge, Son of the North Slope, and the next target of oil developers. My brother and I get nervous when humans occupy the far side of every hill; other people get nervous when an open spot exists on a map or a piece of land remains unexploited. Who was it that said, "In a world of fugitives, the person running in the opposite direction is the mad man?"

Having roughnecked on oil rigs throughout the Southwestern United States, I know that there will never be a National Park dedicated to the beauty and ecological benefits of oil rigs nor will they ever make the endangered species list. Nor will people pay millions of dollars each year just to visit them. The god of our neon culture demands continual sacrifices of our natural heritage and of our children's inheritance, the wilderness, and it never seems appeased nor satiated; it only grows more hungry.

Arriving in Shungnak, I depart the next day for a new adventure in a bizarre and exotic land. Jerry and Deborah try to dissuade me from the childish venture I am about to undertake. I explain to them that at times we do stupid and foolish things, but later in reflection they gather meaning. Giving up trying to talk sense to me, they wish me good fortune and good hunting in my coming journey to the dark side.

Sometimes we act from the heart, throwing reason and caution aside, and move on to fulfill our desires, however absurd they may seem. With that in mind I depart Shungnak and fly directly to New York City to practice law. We all do crazy and foolish things.

Traveling across the tundra pulled by 13 balls of fur at 10 degrees below is a great adventure. Don't sell the family car to go do it; but if the opportunity should slide in your direction don't let it mush on by.

p. Radin

THE DEMPSTER HIGHWAY
1986

P ractising law in New York City never developed into a full love affair, but I did meet my future wife in Washington, D.C. I had returned to the ships and my job of twelve years with the ferries. I had sold my homestead in Tenakee Springs in 1984.

I had been sick in Juneau, Alaska, for a week and was ready for adventure – the Northland was calling. Throwing my gear in my rice buggy (Subaru 4 x 4), I headed out of Juneau in Southeast Alaska on the next ferry to Skagway ninety miles north. A thought cooking in my brain was starting to boil: the Dempster Highway was calling. I remembered the highway on maps snaking out of Dawson and cutting across the Yukon before it slipped into the Northwest Territory, stopping within 70 miles of the Arctic Ocean. My goal was 2,000 miles of gravel road (round trip) from the Pacific Ocean at Skagway to the Arctic Ocean near Univik. I had five days. With a one day layover at Univik (the end of the road), it meant 500 miles a day (ten hours at fifty mph). With a day at Univik, I had one day to spare in case of trouble.

I drove the White Pass out of Skagway. There were actually two passes during the Gold Rush of '98. The Chilkoot was the more famous where the miners went up the Scales, a 40% climb at the end (seen recently in the film "White Fang"). The railroad went through

White Pass in the early 1900s. White Pass was also known as Deadhorse Pass because 3,000 horses died there in 1898 carrying supplies. No one planned for them to live.

In Whitehorse, Yukon Territory, I stopped and searched in vain for a plastic windshield protector. I had plenty of credit in the bank of broken glass. Gravel roads do nothing for windshields. But I could not find a shield screen so I anticipated another sacrifice to the gods of gravel. It was 120 miles to Whitehorse and 400 more to Dawson City (the last part gravel). From there it was 500 miles of unpaved road to Univik.

I camped in Whitehorse and headed out in the morning for the Arctic Ocean. The road from Whitehorse to Dawson follows the ancient river bed of the Yukon River. The Yukon River itself flows to Dawson almost untouched by the road that replaced the Yukon River in the 1950's as the main artery of transportation. This stretch of road crosses many rivers, all flowing to join the Yukon which cuts Alaska in half on its way to the Bering Sea.

I crossed the Stewart River, the Pelly River and others, all good floating rivers with more rapids than the Yukon. In the fall, Natives put on the Pelly and float down to the Yukon River picking up a moose on the way and pulling out at Dawson. One of the rites of spring is watching the ice go out on the rivers, especially the Yukon. The large blocks of ice boom for weeks sliding to the sea. Often, however, the ice jams, creating a dam and flooding. Many towns and cabins get a thorough soaking. Dawson itself has not escaped.

At Pelly Crossing I stopped and talked to the proprietor. He is generally selling land somewhere and I enjoy talking about land whether or not I have money. They are gentle people and religious, but one notes from their appearance that being slender is not a high priority in the bush; nor is it practical. In the northern climate, a person is better off retaining all the heat he can. Slender people lose heat too fast. Fat is not only insulation but a good supply of food as well. Natives, especially Eskimos, have more natural body fat than other people. Though in excellent shape, Natives have little physique because of the extra padding.

These people of the Pelly Crossing showed what was important, a little extra cushion again the cold. One of the proprietor's daughters had recently married. The further one gets from large cities in Alaska and the Yukon, the earlier people tend to marry. Away from cities there is less for a single person to do. Marriage and having a family are the main source of entertainment as it was years ago in the lower 48.

I left Pelly Crossing and drove towards Dawson. I had made this drive many times. For Southeast Alaskans, the Yukon has large towns within 100 miles. The nearest non-Southeast Alaskan town is 700 miles away. Many Southeast Alaskan flee their rain forest to the desert of the Yukon which receives only ten inches of rain a year. Sand dunes exist outside of Carcross, British Columbia.

I turned off at the Dempster Highway just before Dawson City, home of America's Last Great Gold Rush. Ten million in gold came out of Dawson that first year, yet six times that was spent by the stampeders getting it out. Not everyone, in fact only a few, got rich. But the roulette wheels still spin in Dawson and the dancing girls are frolicking for the tourists. Dawson is peculiar because once it housed over 50,000 people and today that number has dropped to 3,000. The number of buildings has dropped as well. Where before a block was covered with buildings, now it may contain only one. Historic Dawson has that vacant look.

I drove 100 miles up the Dempster and camped for the night. I had covered 500 miles that day and tomorrow held 500 more. Luckily, during the Yukon's summer there is no darkness, only twilight.

I awoke at my usual time: 10:00 A.M.; fixed my morning gruel of freeze-dried food and coffee, and hit the road. I noticed not a great number of refueling stations on the highway. The Dempster Highway's original purpose was trucking oil drilling supplies to Inuvik which are then barged down the MacKenzie River 70 miles to the Beaufort Sea and the supply port of Tuk. In winter, truckers drive to Tuk on the Arctic Ocean over the frozen MacKenzie River.

The road was not crowded with RV's, but tourism is growing. If I thought I was daring the unknown on the high road to adventure, my roots were shaken by an ex-greyhound bus turned camper-extraordinaire that lumbered down the highway like a giant beetle. No, the highway is for tourists, including the RV's.

The first stretch of the Dempster goes through the Ogilvie Mountains. The mountains are under 10,000 feet and in the distance rivers wind through them. This territory is one of the last unpolluted and largely unpopulated areas on earth. It has resisted for centuries the encroachment of man. Eventually, every spot on earth offers something to exploit and develop, even the desert and the Arctic (oil is one example).

p. kadin

When I first saw this land, I thought, "Wyoming." The tundra plains spread out from both sides of the road in golden yellow like the high plains of Wyoming. When the peaks are reached in the distance, the tundra turns to stone instead of trees. In Wyoming these would be pines, but here, because of the distance north of the equator, there is rock and little life. At any moment I expected to see a cowboy ride across the plains chasing cattle and rolling his own. He never came, but I still felt in Wyoming.

It was across this land that Amundsen, the future conqueror of the South Pole, raced with his news by dog sled from the Beaufort Sea that he was the first person to sail the Northwest Passage from the Atlantic to the Pacific Ocean. Amundsen chose Eagle in the United States as opposed to Dawson City, 100 miles up stream, because of a telegraph link to the outside.

This is also the land of the Lost Patrol. The Royal Canadian Mounted Police started their ill-fated dog sled trip from Fort McPherson (near the Arctic Ocean) on their annual run to Dawson City. They became lost on the trail when they turned up the wrong canyon. They tried to back-track to Fort McPherson, but weather set in and when their food ran out, so did their luck. They were found thirty miles from the fort. The North can be very unforgiving of mistakes.

Further down the road near Eagle's Nest is where the Mad Trapper of Rat River made his last stand. Hollywood has made several inaccurate films on the life of this crazy but resourceful person. In the more accurate book, he became involved in a squabble over trapping lines on the Rat river. When the Mounties investigated, he shot at them, wounded one, and the chase was on. For several weeks the Mounties chased this renegade through the Yukon and the Northwest Territories. It is possibly the longest pursuit on record by police with dog sleds. The Mounties had more resources and men. The mad trapper had desperation and a devil-may-care attitude. Unable to get adequate supplies the trapper had planned to circle back on his trail after the Mounties had passed to pick up the cache of food they stored on the trail as they traveled.

What the trapper miscalculated was that he was so much faster than the Mounties that he doubled back on his own tracks before the police had gotten that far. When this happened the end was near. The final shoot out occurred near Eagle's Nest on the Dempster Highway. The photos of the dead trapper show a small man, freeze-dried by the Arctic air, and looking strangely like a rat.

I drove for twelve hours that day. The gravel road is shot rock (drilled and fractured with explosives) making it not as smooth as rocks from a stream, but sharp. Being in a hurry is tough on tires. Radial tires at 50 m.p.h. lay partially on their sides around corners. This cuts them to shreds on sharp rocks. I lost two tires on the trip and was not secure limping into the next stop on my emergency spare with half the nylon.

The Mounties made me feel better by daily driving the highways just as they mushed them years ago.

At some point I crossed the Arctic Circle — that imaginary line on the earth marking an area that receives at least one day of no sun and one day of total sun each year.

Over a hill, ribbons of purple flames lined the road in the form of Indian Paintbrush.

Through a mountain pass I entered the Northwest Territories. It was a first for me. I descended a valley and drove to Fort McPherson. The road did not go directly into the town, but I had to see it. I had read the story of the Lost Patrol. There is not much to speak of. The town does not radiate prosperity. One friendly local who had been imbibing a little too much at the local watering hole tried to climb in my car for a ride down the street. He was greatly offended when I did not oblige.

I had crossed the Peel River on a ferry to get to Fort McPherson. I crossed another river, the MacKenzie, on a motorized barge. The

MacKenzie is wide here and attests to the expense necessary to build a bridge that the annual ice break-up could not take out. At this point the Mackenzie was joined by the Red River. The ferry also went to the small town of Red River, sitting on a bluff between the two channels of water.

I was on the last leg to Inuvik, the town built twenty-five years ago by the Canadians as a seat for local government. Another town which at one time was the site for the government is in the MacKenzie delta, but the ground proved too unstable for large buildings. So the Canadians created a new town called Inuvik (which ever way you try to pronounce it, it's wrong).

As I entered on the last stretch to Inuvik, I found myself among evergreen trees that had disappeared miles back. The pines and small lakes put me in Jackson Hole, Wyoming. I was within 100 miles of the Arctic Ocean, but I saw Wyoming.

I also noticed, as I drove the highway, that every windshield was cracked. When I blew one too many tires on the way back, I hitched a ride with someone who had a cracked windshield and who said that the first thing you did with a new car was throw a rock at the windshield so that you never had to worry about it again.

Arriving in the town of Inuvik, I took up residence at the campground. The ubiquitous mosquito showed that it treated locals and tourists alike; there was no discrimination: they bit everyone. They were certainly non-union, as they worked all hours and even overtime. I protested that I only supported union shops. They flew past my protests fearing not my wrath. In the confines of my dome tent, I dealt the few trapped blood-suckers a startling vengeance!

The next day in Univik was devoted to tourism. I took in the sights, like a good tourist, which included the three story high igloo-shaped church. But my eyes wandered to things not on the tourist list — such as the sewer pipes coming out above ground because of the permafrost (permanently frozen ground) to a collection box where it led to other pipes. In oil rich Barrow, Alaska, they built underground tunnels to carry their sewage and utilities. I also noticed the local Natives, sunbathing in the eighty degree weather. Four times, I was told, Univik had recorded the highest temperature in Canada, only seventy miles from the Arctic Ocean.

I drove down to the MacKenzie River, that great waterway of the Northwest Territories. What I saw was only a branch since this was the delta and most rivers spread out before they hit the sea.

This arm was a good sized river. I threw my inflatable raft in the MacKenzie River and had a short float. While I was paddling, a one hundred foot Canadian Coast Guard buoy tender pulled in and sucked the water level down two feet in docking by the void it left in the water behind it.

Locals told stories of seventy foot waves on the MacKenzie during storms. The buoy tender looked like it was made for huge seas. The local canoes were not made for flat water, but had a large bow with the stern squared off and fitted with a motor.

I had my fun in the kayak and then got out of the glacial melt water. A major expedition on the MacKenzie was still on the back burner.

I sent my bride-to-be in Washington, D.C. a Northwest Territories postcard displaying huge icebergs. Large icebergs are rare in the Arctic Ocean because there is little precipitation to make glaciers on land which calve in the ocean as icebergs. Big land born icebergs in the Arctic are highly prized by scientists as a stable base on which to float and do research. The sea ice is not as thick and thus not as stable.

I wanted to see the Arctic Ocean. I had seen two oceans and I wanted another on my list. I had flown over it, but that didn't count. I made arrangements with a local company to fly out with other tourists (some from my future homestead town of Petersburg, Alaska). We took off that afternoon in a floatplane across the seventy miles to the Arctic Ocean. I have flown in many floatplanes during my ten years of homesteading in Southeast Alaska, but never have I climbed in a plane to see the pilot studying a map with such intensity.

I am scared by many things and a pilot who during the entire flight does not take his eyes off the map in his lap is one of them. How would one feel to climb into an airliner only to have the pilot say, "Has anybody ever gone here before?"

We flew over the 70 miles of rounded lakes and muskeg to the oil production port of Tuk (it is actually a much longer name but it never stuck with me). The pilot did find the town, for that he gets credit, but he couldn't locate the floatplane ramp to disembark. We flew around for 10-15 minutes dodging helicopters before he put down on the water; but then nobody on the radio could tell us our location. We cruised around on our airplane floats looking for a place to disembark. Finally we took to the air again and spotted the airplane float dock. By this time a storm was rolling in from the Arctic Ocean.

The ice cap which was 60 miles offshore was no place to be seen. The pilot now said we could not land because the storm would trap us for the night. I cared little for his arguments. I wanted to see this strange town with its port full of barges and oil exploration equipment. But the pilot prevailed. However, we were now, because of our unscheduled wanderings, too short on fuel to fly back by the paid-for route up the MacKenzie River.

He got us back and we were only charged half for the experience. Never climb into a plane where the pilot has a map in his lap and a look of confusion on his face. Undoubtedly, the airplane company during the busy tourist season grabs any pilot it can from southern Canada and throws him in the seat to drive the tourists crazy. The hardy people from Pete's town asked if I would try it again tomorrow. I knitted my brow at them. Besides, I had two days to drive another 1,000 miles of gravel road.

The Dempster is a fun highway for those short on adventure and long on tires. Try it; you'll like it.

p. radin

HOMESTEADING IN ALASKA:
THE DREAM LIVES ON
1987

Beware of all enterprises that require new clothes.

— Henry David Thoreau

My career in the law had ended for the second time. I bid fond farewell and adieu to the Bored of Veterans Appeals – a great institution with many fine attorneys whom I decided could hold the world together without me.

I had finished an internship with the Board of Veterans Appeals and had the option of staying on as a full time attorney. But, my wife and I had decided that I would return to work on the ships of the Alaska Marine Highway in the summer and that after our schooling and medical treatment in Washington, D.C. eventually we would move permanently to my "principle place of abode" in Alaska.

My wife and I had been married the previous summer. I had had a person construct the shell to my second homestead in Alaska. This second homesite through the great state of Alaska was located on a serpentine channel amidst the Tongass National Forest in Southeast Alaska. A sandy beach on the Pacific Ocean was our front yard and the street in front was the Wrangell Narrows: one of the main arteries for vessels of Southeast Alaska.

I had acquired the right to homestead the land in 1982, but I had not pursued serious development because I was still involved in a fight over my first homestead. Never divide your forces: either in battle or homesteading. In 1984 I ended my affair with my federal homesite claim which was originally signed into law by the Great Emancipator himself, Abraham Lincoln. For two years I drifted, unable to decide to commit myself to another ten years in the bush. My first homestead had taken ten years which was nine years and 11 months longer than I had planned. Thirty years of aging squeezed into a single decade was becoming harder and harder to justify.

I could not make the quantum leap until I married a choral singer from Washington, D.C. and saw Alaska slipping forever from my grasp. Needing an anchor that would always draw me back, I threw a hook into my homestead. I hired help to put in the foundation and raise the roof up on a small cabin, 16 feet by 16 feet with a loft (an upper floor which is limited by the pitch of the roof). One only has to spend years in the mud and rain getting the roof up to realize that no one ever died of laughter doing it. During our honeymoon, on a beautiful Southeast Alaskan day, we journeyed to Alaska and visited the new cabin and homesite.

Thus, the following summer, after wintering over in D.C., I quit my legal job with few regrets and headed to Seattle, Washington where my ship of the poor man's cruise line, the Alaska Marine Highway, was receiving final touches before going on the run in late May.

I had a few items I needed to support my second coming to the bush: a VW camper, boat, engine, cabinets, sink, closet, flooring, generator, shower, storage shed, plus a few hundred miscellaneous tools and materials. A week later like a giant beetle I lumbered aboard the vessel departing from Seattle for Southeast Alaska with my old, but newly purchased VW bus, loaded to the gunnels (the top railing of a boat).

I worked a week on/week off the cruise ship which allowed time to homestead in remote areas. My new bride was coming in June and I had to render the place more livable. She didn't mind talking about camping so long as she never had to do it.

Upon arriving in Juneau, I was off for a week and proceeded to locate the boat which I had not found in Seattle. The type of boat I desired was a Boston Whaler which was heavy, but unsinkable; one

p. kadir

had only to pull the plug out when one went away and the water drained out (it's all foam like a styrofoam cup). Since I would be away for weeks with no one to bail my boat, a self-bailer was crucial.

I found a good, but used boat, and the seller threw in the trailer as well. I had bought a new motor because you never take used motors to the bush — repairs are difficult if not impossible. A used boat is different.

I loaded my boat on the ferry to Petersburg, the Norwegian fishing community where my homesite was located. I pushed the boat and trailer on the ferry by hand since I had no trailer hitch which also meant I had no way of hauling my boat out the road to the boat dock in Petersburg. Alaska constantly presents insurmountable problems, but also unforeseeable solutions.

At the Petersburg ferry terminal I met several locals knocking off half a rack of beer in the parking lot who had a trailer hitch on their truck. It was the wrong size but for a twenty dollar fee they went into town and bought the right size; put it on their truck and hauled me out the road. At Papkee's Landing, the public dock for people who lived down the channel, the men helped me put my boat in the water and even started the engine. I gave them the trailer since I had no plans for it. I proceeded to overload my boat and started off on the six mile trip to my cabin with a motor that was too small but still too large for the boat by Coast Guard standards. I landed at my homestead and hauled the materials up to the cabin. It took several trips down the channel to complete the task and, towards the end, I was promising myself that some day I would learn how to handle such a boat.

One of the problems with water transportation in Southeast Alaska is finding a good parking spot. With 20 foot tides and a large tidal flat in front of my homesite I had to devise a means of keeping my boat afloat yet accessible. That first night I pulled my boat up high above the tide line. I will long remember that night of the long day, nodding out at the beach while sipping Scotch and smoking a cigar, making sure the tide was going out and my boat safe.

The next day, I devised a haul-out line which is a rope attached to a buoy (anchored in deep water) by a pulley through which the line circles and then completes the loop through a pulley on the beach. The boat is tied to the rope and hauled out to deep water. When needed, the boat is pulled back to shore. Theoretically perfect, it is not always practical. The boat was in the heavy tidal current which swept through the channel in both directions twice a day, fouling my lines with seaweed and dragging the boat up and down the channel. Finally, I simply tied my boat to the anchored float and reached it by kayak. I owned three kayaks and had a good Eskimo roll. One never knows what ability may become important in homesteading.

I had to make the place as habitable as possible for my city-oriented wife. We would never have pressurized water, a flush toilet, electricity, or phone, and, for a while, no shower. Though the situation might be primitive, it did not have to be a dirty trapper's cabin either. I started putting in the cabinets and counters. I used an empty Scotch bottle as a roller to lay the linoleum. In the bush, improvisation is a necessity. One can never plan for everything and the store required a six hour trip. One uses what is available and creativity is a plus.

The next time off the ship I brought my new bride out to the homestead. The first days were a little intense. She had to cook over a barbecue grill because the propane burners were not installed. No sink or counter, plus eating on the porch because I was working inside, did not help. When the microscopic, biting No-See-Um bugs became particularly bad, Carleen said she could not live like this. I was taken back. Compared to how I had lived at my first homestead this was Club Med. We had done what we could to make the place habitable and we only had money enough for materials and had to do the work ourselves. Our peace and happiness swung on the hinge of fate until more amenities began to appear.

It had been an impossible proposition. Could a woman from a big eastern city find happiness in the Alaskan outback, if only for the summer? Raised in a small West Virginia town, my wife's big city habits had been well grafted to her humble origins. We never bothered to calculate the impossibilities, because love loathes reason. It was a gamble, at best. Eventually, after the kitchen, the gas stove, the shower, shelving, etc. began to appear, Carleen was more able to accept the wilderness setting. Make them desperate, then they'll appreciate anything!

She discovered that lack of a daily shower did not turn one into a troll. Somehow the absence of TV, phone, electricity was not terminal.

I had as little reason to be out in the bush as she did. I neither hunted nor fished a great deal as do most people who venture to the wilderness. My reason for existing in the bush is to escape the intrusions of our electronic world.

The world invents "time saving" items which supposedly increase efficiency and production and thus bring greater happiness. However, progress is an illusion. It is such because every time we create something new, we create a new standard by which to judge it. This is similar to the problem of being unable to measure both the speed and location of an electron, because to measure the speed we effect its position. Another example of this phenomenon is the carp or goldfish (by another name), which always grows to the size of its container. Thus, no matter how large the container, it never has any more room.

Thus we have eliminated or reduced numerous diseases that killed and crippled humans, but who remembers all those crippling diseases any more? In the past, what many people hoped for was simply to be able to feed, shelter, and raise their family without death knocking at the door. Who today in the "me" generation would this satisfy? We have created miracles, but those miracles no longer satisfy. We must have more.

Each new solution brings another problem. Automobiles have created more problems than they have solved.

A great deal of our time is spent protecting, defending, cleaning, insuring, displaying, buying, and deposing of our material goods, and it takes 30 years of education to understand and operate most of them.

The great beauty of the Great Alone is that there is nothing to do but survive. Water must be hauled; wood chopped; supplies brought in; baths taken at night in the ocean; lanterns filled for light, etc.

My life and energy in the bush are devoted to doing those things which have been eliminated in modern society. Yet that brings me the greatest pleasure. I do that which is necessary for survival and not because of pressure to conform with others. The world bombards us with messages that turn luxuries into necessities. Is it really necessary that we wear different, new, and stylish clothes each day? The pressure to meet the expectations of many anonymous people disappears at the cabin. We are not so aware in the bush that we have numerous meaningless standards to maintain.

This is not to say I do not enjoy the city – I do. The homesite acts as a foil to city life. In both, I am derived of benefits of the other and can better appreciate both. As Peter Beardsley, a New York socialite and African photographer said, "The experience of New York is so much heightened against the backdrop of Africa."

I don't go out to the bush to be alone. I go out there to be with people: where there is much less competing for my time and attention. Besides being great company, my wife insists upon good food. The high point of my year is sitting down to a meal of salmon after a day's work on the cabin and nightly swim in the ocean. She has brought classical music to the wilderness in both her voice and tapes. Though it may seem conversation might falter with only two people, we never seem to run out of interesting things to experience and relate.

During the day when the sun is out, my wife lays out on the sandy beach in her swimming suit on a lounge chair. Except for the rubber boots and bug spray located nearby, one would think she was in the Bahamas. The tow boats toot their horns as they go by and tourists on the passing small cruise ships and ferries never imagined that this is what homesteading in Alaska is all about.

p. Radin

MY FLIGHT FROM
THE GREAT CYCLOPS
1987

When it comes to television, I am illiterate.

— Colman McCarthy

As a child I grew up on Walt Disney, Davy Crockett, and the television set. My favorite day was Friday when school was out and Walt Disney was on. I had a hard time deciding which was my favorite day when Disney moved to Sunday night.

I was, in fact, the first generation of television addicts. Born in 1950, nearly at the same time that TV made its debut, I was raised with it as part of my environment. We grew together or possibly we grew separately. I spent a great part of youth lying in front of the TV watching the prime shows: *Hogan's Heroes, Gunsmoke, Bonanza, McHale's Navy,* etc. The only people who watched more TV than I were my cousins from Iraq who visited once and who did not have a great deal of TV nor westerns in Iraq.

Through junior high and part of high school, I thought the TV was my friend and I devoted long periods to that friendship. By my later years of high school and college, however, the relationship was definitely on the ropes with little chance of going the distance. I was away at college and on the road a good deal of the time and far, far too many things were happening to give any time to TV.

At first it was not a conscious rejection of the tube; it was simply that more important things had taken its place — like when girls took the place of sand lot baseball. For several years during college I was on the road wandering from place to place, college to college, country to country. There was little TV along the way. Although, when I was living in foreign countries and studying foreign languages, television would probably have been a help.

I do remember a few other times (such as after my return from Europe to Utah while working on drilling rigs in Salt Lake City) that I would stay up to watch the late movie.

In law school, I was hooked on Johnny Carson with my roommate who convinced me of Johnny's virtues. In later years I would come out from my homestead at Tenakee in Southeast Alaska to watch Johnny Carson — though in later years he paled.

I refused to take a TV from my grandmother when she offered it to me and my roommate at law school. Instead we had to rent one. Years later when I returned to law school, I borrowed the same TV and watched Johnny again.

But through the years TV had become an enemy. As I saw more and more people watching it I became more and more disinterested. Possibly living in the Alaskan bush put a different slant to my life or caused me to think too much.

The bush was the one place which remained untarnished by the great one-eyed Cyclops, television. When I arrived in Tenakee (an isolated Southeast Alaskan fishing village) in 1974, there was no such thing as TV. The closest entertainment approaching TV was the local movie theater where the owner showed only the movies the town could afford (which weren't many). The battered old movie theater was called the Shamrock and years before was the town's red-light district. I thought I would burst with laughter and joy sitting down in the rickety seats in a building that swayed over the water. I watched old westerns with the local town folk while munching popcorn and slurping soda pop. That was the big Saturday night movie in the city of Tenakee for which the whole town turned out.

In the town of Tenakee, my friend Chuck was a Texan who had come to Alaska to hunt bear and work on the oil rigs. He was over six feet tall, partially bald, and big like most oil workers, though he was becoming stouter with age. He switched from oil rigs to running heavy equipment in his later years. When he was in the bucks as was I, I would go down to his place two or three times a week to cook dinner and polish off some whiskey. There was nothing to entertain us so we had to entertain ourselves. We talked and shouted and drank and cooked for hours on end. Most of what we said probably made little sense, especially after the first few drinks.

When I was home from the ferries for a week during a summer while in law school, we went out at six o'clock in the evening and pulled crabs from Chuck's crab pots and then cracked them open and dumped them in a large pot of boiling water. We melted a whole pan of butter and had previously picked up a case of mountain-fresh Rainier from the store. We could hardly eat the thirty crabs so we handed them out to people as they passed down the trail where we dined in the summer. At about midnight we staggered down to the local hot springs bath. Later we would pledge to meet at six the next day to go for more crabs and our six hour dining experience.

With the coming of the great one-eyed god, this ended. When the town of Tenakee got its great dish to speak to the stars (the telephone satellite dish) it also received TV and its Alaskan Public Broadcasting. All fueled by oil revenues.

The first to die was the movie theater. It lasted one week. There were better quality movies in one night of TV than the theater could show in a month. Next to go were the bars where one could sit down and get something to eat and drink or just chew the fat. Now the two bars in town began to be partly dominated by spirits of TV. Possibly the bartenders turned them on so as not to hear the local bickering.

The conversations between Chuckles and myself slowly dropped off. Maybe there were other reasons. Possibly I was becoming more and more bitter and disgruntled about my homestead and less open. Conceivably Chuck was becoming bitter with his lot when it became difficult to find work and he seldom could leave the town. But the dinners came to an end nonetheless. No longer would we sit and swap lies in the fastness of the castle keep — throwing down a shot of brandy, tossing noodles against the wall to see if they were done, and arguing over who was going to cook and who would clean up. The necessity of entertaining ourselves was gone. We no longer had to work at conversation and intercourse. It was all taken care of for us by the great One-Eyed Monster. Whenever I walked into Chuck's house the Cyclops would be screaming in my face. One does not have to converse when the TV is on. It takes over. It removed the necessity of entertaining ourselves. Throughout Tenakee this phenomenon took place. No one had to go out to be entertained. One could stay in his own place alone and get it done.

Fortunately, with our affluent society that allows many people to live alone (such as my parents and grandmother), it also gives them something to create the atmosphere of people: TV. My main problem with TV is that it is used to displace what is the basis of human happiness: human communication and interaction. After food, shelter, and safety, the greatest generator of happiness is human relations. Few people are like male polar bears, almost always alone, wandering the dark polar ice cap for food. With all the material goods possible, few people would survive cut off completely from people.

The greatest creator of happiness, relations with others, requires effort and work. Television has contrived to make it easier, but it doesn't work. How many people turn on the television in their home to create the atmosphere of people being there? We get the taste of human interaction but there is no nourishment. How many families watch TV because it is easier than interacting? Television doesn't ignore us, anger us, require effort to interact, or belittle us. It is always there to offer beautiful people whom we feel we are relating with, but we aren't.

How many people have moved out on their own so that they don't have to bother with interfacing and communicating with someone? There is little pay back by deriving relationships from the boob

p. Radin

tube. We don't get the feedback from electronic furniture that is essential for human self-worth and development. Many of us are social midgets because we took the short-cut of the electronic pacifier instead of doing our homework of human inter-relations along with its pains and burdens.

Communication is truly amazing. There are kids above the Arctic Circle who through TV satellite know more about Michael Jackson and the latest rock and roll groups than their counterparts in New York City. Their own culture goes sadly neglected however. Of the hundreds of bush communities in Alaska offered TV, only one decided it did not want TV interfering with their lives.

On another plane, TV is as polluting as smoking. It does not cause a chemical reaction in our nose like a cigarette which offends people more and more these days, but it does provide light patterns (visual) and vibrations (sound) which are received by people in its vicinity that cause distractions, interference, and revulsion (murder, graphic sex, advertisement, game shows, etc.). Pollution (unwanted and undesirable items) by light and sound can be more offensive than by chemicals (at least chemicals don't try to convince you that beautiful people drink Budweiser).

But back to our story. I was becoming paranoid of television. It had reached me in the bush after many years. It had leaped across continents and oceans to descend upon me in the wilderness. I admit I once even watched it in my cabin one day in Tenakee. It kept me from feeling lonely and helped me work better for a day. But then I realized what a crutch it was and threw it out.

When I was out of Tenakee, I saw TVs in the bars. They followed me into grocery stores where they tried to sell me wine. They were even in the shopping carts. Wherever I turned, I met the unblinking gaze of the Cyclops who was there to tell me how to think, act, and spend my money and always, to offend me.

I felt safe on the cruise ships on which I worked in Southeast Alaska. Those moving cities did not carry a satellite to bring in all that electronic garbage. But the Cyclops was not to be denied its daily meal of the human mind. One day videos appeared. In the eighties, the ships became littered with them. They crawled and slithered into every crew mess. A crew member would stick a movie in the video player, and then leave and everybody else would have to suffer through it. The noise and bloody, naked bodies being thrown through the air were distracting. The conversations of the crew which were free flowing before now had to fight against the constant influence of the boob tube. I could see I was fighting a losing battle.

But being resourceful, I obtained another homestead not close to any town so I would not have to deal with any dishes and broadcasts. There I do feel safe for awhile. In my other homes in the city, I try to keep the television in an area where one has to work to use it. How people find time for TV is beyond me. However, how I could spend so much time as a kid watching the tube is also beyond my grasp.

I continue to flee from the unblinking gaze of the Great Cyclops, but I know I "blow a futile horn." I see the world of the future decorated with these one-eyed monsters instructing humans how to better their entire lives through sex, violence, and human isolation.

p.Radin

THE FINE ART OF JUMPING OFF CLIFFS (OR ANYTHING ELSE FOR THAT MATTER)

1988

*If it doesn't kill me, it will
probably make me stronger*

— Nietzsche

N ow for something completely different. It doesn't have a lot to do with Alaska but the tale must be told.

I looked down through the branches at one of the Seven Sacred Pools near Hana on Maui, Hawaii. Sixty feet below, a deep blue oval pond was carved by the river between volcanic cliffs. Then I was air born. To this day, I believe it was almost an unconscious act when I took a running jump, planted my foot on a low branch of a tree and propelled myself into space.

I cleared the first set of trees and branches and an outcropping of rocks. I cleared a last set of branches prior to splash down. But the running jump and launch through the trees had thrown my balance off. As I plummeted from the heavens both automatic gyros (my arms) kicked in, but did little good. My feet hit first -- that was the good part since landing on my stomach, side, or back has always been a negative experience. However, as I entered into more solid forms of matter, my right shoulder, being lower than the left, was forced violently upwards as if my hand had caught on an invisible hook in the sky.

I sank deep in the water, then floated upwards with the bubbles. I had injured myself again. It was not the first nor would it be the last time I violated my body in games with gravity. When you play with fire, getting burnt is part of the experience.

I fluttered my way like a gaffed fish to a rock people were spectating on. Climbing out of the water, I pulled a bottle of elixir out of my pack and proceeded to lessen the pain. One lady asked, "Do you do that all the time?" I replied, "Yes." The other people ignored me, possibly fearing whatever I had might be catching.

But I had planned well. It was the end of my vacation in Hawaii. I had but a day left (actually my vacation was extended three days to recover from pulled muscles in my neck and shoulder.) I had ruined too many vacations by jumping off the tallest cliff the first day. I had grown wiser in my latter years and now left the "banzai" cliffs until the end.

Rumor has it that I started jumping off house roofs at age five. Maybe that is why I am so short. Frankly, I deny it, but I have always had a love affair with jumping. People who had not seen me in 30 years remembered me solely because of my constant jumping off chairs and tables as a child. Probably my best jump to hard ground was in Italy during my second year of college when I leaped from a 14 foot high balcony, out six feet to the grass below (my greatest accomplishment that year).

I do not wish to defend jumping or even try to explain it. If you do it you love it; if you don't, then you spend less time in the hospital. My purpose here is to celebrate with the few who draw joy "...in leaving the surly bonds of earth to touch the face of God." I leave the analyzing to the analysts; the deploring to the deplorists; and the questioning to whomever. I wish solely to glorify it to those who glory in it and maybe give encouragement and a few pointers.

Ski jumping has been a part of my game with one of the four forces of the universe: gravity. I have broken three pair of wood skis and bent one metal pair; torn ligaments and tendons in the left ankle and knee and broken the bone in between (all in separate accidents); put a ski pole into my hand; cut a gash on my

Chicken Heart, South Fork of the Turtle River, by Jerry Dixon

chin; and smashed and enlarged the size of my nose and upper lip impossibly out of proportion. All injuries were related to ski jumping. Bruce, a faithful friend of mine, has assisted in removing my remains from the hill so many times that he feels half St. Bernard:

"Get the good toboggan this time, Bruce. The last one you procured for me isn't worth mentioning. And get me a lady ski patrol this time. Men never give enough sympathy. I work hard to break my leg. I expect the same of you."

"What I appreciate about this, Mike," replied Bruce as he undid my twisted leg once, "is that you're learning. You managed not to break your leg this time until the last day of the ski season, on the last run, 100 yards from the bottom. This did not cut into your ski year at all."

"That's why I choose to annihilate myself with you, Bruce. You appreciate the finer points. Now get me a cute ski patrol person who can deal with my wounds properly."

Inverted aerials (flips) were the worst thing that ever happened to ski jumping. As soon as skiers started breaking their necks doing stupid flips, the ski areas knocked down every bump larger than an ant hill. Ski jumping has almost become a lost art.

I never went into competition jumping. I enjoyed the simple jumps with a rough landing, no out run and possible destruction on the other end. I preferred "wild" jumps or natural hills exploited by skiers and to pay my dues at the other end. However, years have passed now and my back is not what it used to be. Many times I preferred not to go skiing because I knew once on the hill I could not stop from jumping. To do thirty or forty feet off a natural jump on to flat ground leaves me in traction. Maybe I'm glad they destroyed all the bumps. But to the jumpers of the world -- keep going for glory!

One of my best jumping buddies, Jim, is an ex-parachutist who had 500 jumps when he turned in his chute. Possibly too many of his friends got 100% free-fall with no chute time and he figured his number was coming up. I tried four jumps myself and I am loath to admit it, but I was scared. The fun was gone. The margin of error was too lean, besides having to wait for the wind to die in hot, dirty shacks surrounded by flat and ugly scenery. To paraphrase another: the position was ridiculous, the pleasure momentary, and the consequences eternal (though of course this might be said of all jumping).

The difference with the jumping in this article whether it be hard ground, ski, or cliff jumping is called: fail safe. Unless a person is completely reckless or intoxicated, the chance of death or serious permanent injury (mayhem) is slight if not non-existent. Jumping from 20 feet into deep water even if in the most abandoned way will only produce discomfort. Ski jumping if kept under 10 feet in height and 30 feet in distance (excluding flips) will at most produce a broken leg (and with equipment of today not even that; most of my ski injuries came from earlier, less safe, and less forgiving equipment).

Hard Ground Jumping requires a little more skill and a good roll, but under ten feet is fairly safe. With parachuting, hang gliding, BASE (jumping with a parachute from less than a 1000 feet) etc., one mess up and you buy the farm. That's the difference with the jumping exalted in this diatribe: there is a limit to damage liability.

Although Hard Ground Jumping has been important and skiing will always be close to me, in liquid H_2O I excelled. There I broke new ground, or rather water. I started off diving in a pool and working on flips (the double flip I could never claim).

One of my first baptisms of fire was off freeways in Rupert, Idaho in the glory days of youth during the Summer of Love of 1967. My cousin and I worked in Salt Lake City, Utah, during the week and on the weekend headed for his home in the little Idaho farm town of Rupert to seek out the farm girls and the greatest expanse of irrigation canals in the United States. The girls were beautiful but the canals were just as good. With the tow rope tied to an automobile, we skied at speeds of 70 m.p.h., parallel to the road, along a mile of straight canal. Then on the flip-side of the run with the car on the opposite bank, we jumped off a bridge four feet to the water and slalom skied on the glass like surface. Later we swam the chute: 10,000 cfs (cubic feet per second) through a cement trough, 40 feet wide, that exploded into Class III white water on the boulders below. Then to the freeway where we raced across the lanes and leaped from the bridge before the highway patrol could spot us. One instructional time while stupidly diving, I hit head first in six feet of water and earned an inch cut on my head. It was a lesson that I could have been paralyzed for life.

Another time, while posing for a picture, I dove at an alpine lake from 15 feet. I luckily turned up at the last moment and only my chest bares the scars from the rocks on the bottom. That is another example of failure to gauge or check the depth and of stupidity in diving.

Several years ago my main diving buddy, Jim, and I were basking in the sun and diving off an incomplete freeway over a lake in Seattle, Washington. It was 37 feet of pure freedom. Jim was built like a modern Prometheus and excelled at the swan dive. We fell and dove off the expressway all day in the sun. Finally, I decided to try the old one and a half. I had missed it a year earlier when I attempted one off a dock in a remote fishing village in Alaska. Pulling out of the tuck too late, my legs came over and compressed the muscles in my back. It took a year to recover.

I had to get back into doing flips from heights or forever lose the courage. Unfortunately, the only place available was 37 feet high. I lost it on the first turn. My mind went blank. I had no idea where I was and I refused to open my eyes to find out. I saved myself by doing a full flip with my eyes closed! More amazing to myself was that I had never done just a flip from over 20 feet. Otherwise, all I did was knock my guts up into my throat. But even that felt good after a brush with oblivion, and we proceeded to celebrate my deliverance. As we did, a black person did a full back flip off the expressway.

The funny part of this particular story happened the next day as we were diving at Chicken Heart on the South Fork of the Toutle River. Beautiful volcanic cliffs edged the milky green glacial stream flowing from Mt. St. Helens.

Try as I might, I could not do a one and a half flip (from over 20 feet): that day all I could perform were full flips – and I am terrible at full flips! Amazing things happen to you while pushing the limits. Some time later I started doing 1½ flips again from over 20 feet and lost the ability to do a full flip from that height. Jim was in fine form that day and I have a painting of us diving at the 30 foot level in a beautiful day of a beautiful time (a year later Mt. St. Helens, in a volcanic orgasm, blew the area into oblivion).

Tips on Hard Ground Jumping:
1. Have a good roll (that is what absorbs the shock).
2. Heavy boots have been known to give greater support to ankles (such as with smokejumpers).
3. Remember the more the weight, the greater the force on the ankles, knees, etc. (smaller people have an advantage over larger folks).

Tips on Ski jumping:
1. Learn to ski.
2. Man made jumps, even thought larger, are often easier than natural ones.
3. Good luck finding any jumps after the era of inverted aerials (flips).

Tips on jumping and diving:

1. Always check the depth first by wading into the water, swimming to where you are going to jump, putting your hand over your head, and submerging yourself until your hand is gone. That should give you 7-8 feet which is good for a 20 foot jump. Have at least 12 feet if you're diving. Paralysis is forever.
2. Always jump first even if you plan to dive to give yourself a feel for the height.
3. Wear tennis shoes for hard landings (even the water hurts your feet when jumping from 20 feet) and for extractions from rocky places.
4. Jumping is safer than diving and just as dignified.
5. When jumping, raise your hands above your head just before entering to prevent smacking the water at 40 m.p.h. with your arms.
6. Diving with a partner is preferable over diving alone (better still if someone has experience in jumping).
7. Be creative.

I recommend diving or jumping off of cruise ships, Mexican cliffs, Italian bridges, Iraqi bridges, sandstone cliffs (Lake Powell, Utah), piers, cable bridges (Main Salmon River, Idaho), and trees (Triangle Lake, Oregon.)

One of the firsts that still remain in creative jumping is diving off a glacier. In one of the great ironies of my life, as I floated down the Alsek River in Canada past 20 foot cliffs of solid ice at Lowell glacier, my mind failed to realize the possibilities. The faces of glaciers are notoriously unstable as that is where they disintegrate. For some reason, in this icy lake through which the Alsek River flowed, the glacial front was extremely stable. There was 20 feet of free fall which was difficult to find anywhere. That was a sad day in my career.

To the jumper/divers of the world–keep jumping. Though diving lessons are not illegal, I pride myself on never taking lessons except the hard way: teach yourself and enjoy the pain and pleasure.

Keep diving, but remember, be careful: paralysis is forever and death is even longer.

PARADISE RE-VISITED: KAYAKING THE SAN JUAN ISLANDS
(1988)

Anybody can be good in the country.

— Oscar Wilde

During a summer weekend in the Pacific Northwest, endless possibilities for adventures climbed, rafted, and water-skied through my mind, but kayaking the San Juan Islands paddled to the forefront.

Being at heart a "bag" lady or person, I had numerous amounts of adventure supporting material stuffed, layered, sorted and stored in my back pack, and in my back-up back pack or my auxiliary overflow bag. I was departing my wintering grounds along the polluted waters of Washington, D.C.'s Potomac river (where dead fish float three blocks from the EPA headquarters) for my summer feeding grounds in Alaska. During my packing operation, my wife had seen my climbing shoes laying out and had locked them up. In trying to have children, she figured a live husband would do better (we had been having problems conceiving). But mountaineering, kayaking, rafting, etc. were well supported in my bags of instant adventure.

119

p. kadir

I was working in Seattle on what promised to be a sunny, beautiful week-end and I was badly in need of spiritual re-fueling, self-healing and general debauchery of laying in the sun, drinking scotch and reading.

Having flown in from Washington, D.C. on the way to my ship, conveniently or prophetically as I exited the Sea-Tac airport in my rented "global warming device" (automobile), a kayak rental agency appeared off my port bow. I steered my vessel to an easy docking. Within a few minutes I was the proud lessor of a sea-kayak with accessories for paddling through the mystical Islands of San Juan.

I unfortunately had to spend a day earning a living on the cruise ship laid-up in the shipyard that employed me. Before my departure northward to the magical isles, I returned Friday to retrieve my gallant water-steed. I discovered the price of rental did not include a car rack. Many kayakers must start paddling immediately from Sea-Tac Airport, born on by desire, not needing the basic necessity of water!

After an inflationary fee for a rack, I drove north 90 miles from the isthmus of Seattle to the port of Anacortes where the ferry departed to the archipelago of San Juan. While working the engine room on cruise ships, one of my jobs entailed recording the sea water temperatures for the engines' cooling manifold. In the San Juans the temperature climbed ten degrees over other waters in the Inside Passage (some people attribute this temperature to volcanic activity under the area).

The San Juan Islands lay in a rain shadow of the mountains on the Olympic peninsula and Vancouver Island. Coming from the ocean in the west, clouds drop rain on the mountains rather than on the low lying islands. The land, 20,000 years ago, was under a sea of ice which melted reducing the weight and allowing the land to rise. Though the islands are covered with evergreens, the moisture they receive is less than the surrounding mountainous rain forests.

Vancouver Island of Canada is driven like a wedge into the "U" shaped northwest corner of Washington with the Olympic Peninsula on one end of the "U" and Anacortes on the other. In the middle of the wedge and surrounded on all sides by mountains are the San Juan Islands.

I arrived at the ferry dock to the islands near midnight. Being in the western U.S., I refused to pay to camp; that was only an eastern U.S. rule even if I camped in a 7-11 parking lot. Eventually, I stumbled on a free state campground, threw up my tent, and collapsed into darkness.

Nature's alarm clock, the sun, had me up at 8:00 am and well roasted. Thanks be to that morning star, because I could never had done it alone. I packed and sorted my various bags as much as I could endure. When I arrived at the ferry dock, the few cars of the night before must have been VW Rabbits because they had reproduced enough to fill the parking lot of Disneyland. Obviously, the San Juans were not a local secret.

I was drawing heavily on my credit of blessings from the Bank of Religious Observance, because I was late but so was the ferry. I found a handicapped parking space close to the terminal and un-loaded my kayak (limping all the time). Then I drove half a mile to park on the only available spot: an oversized sidewalk. Rental cars seem to go where I would never take my car! Then I jogged back to the ferry terminal.

The wheels of gold I rented to transport my craft on board the ferry attached tentatively at one end and provided great amusement for the other passengers. Those kayak rental people must have been breaking ribs in laughter over my deployment of their self-destructing wheels. I am a Class III white-water kayaker but I was sadly in need of extensive training in kayak-land-wheel transport.

Arriving at the island of Orcas, I carried my craft off the ferry and launched from a private dock. I carefully folded the five dollar receipt for the privilege of entering the water and placed it in safe keeping to use during my next bowel movement. I paddled off into large swells crashing against the dock from power boats. I kept an eye out for other crafts of my kind, but kayakers seemed on the endangered species list.

The San Juan Islands are beautiful. There are four or five large islands and numerous lessor atolls and reefs. Treed largely with evergreens the islands lie low and gather little water or clouds similar to the Bahamas in the Caribbean. With the sun exploding in the sky, this paradise should be condo heaven except the lack of water keeps down development. Most of the shoreline is pristine, though well decorated with "No Trespass" signs.

At one point I passed between Orcas Island and Chase Island through a narrow slot. At this pinched point, I was floating with a six m.p.h. current. Waves stood in the passage as the ocean rolled through. In a river waves stand still while the water moves. In the ocean the water stands still while the wave moves. In this particular case, the ocean was acting like a river until a power boat went through and then it acted like a river and an ocean with standing waves added to moving ones; thus my concern.

I waited until I saw no boats and shot the gap. I cleared it without having to practice my Eskimo roll in a sea kayak which is difficult at best. Sea kayaks are more stable than white-water kayaks, but once rolled they are harder to up-right again. White-water kayaks are cramped quarters offering greater control while sea kayaks have leg room designed for hours of paddling without stopping (at the price of losing the roll).

I pressed on through utopia, a modern day Shangri-la. Hundred thousand dollar homes peaked out from trees over looking deep green seas. An unidentified evergreen with smooth bark stretched exotically for the heavens.

I headed for Jones Island, a state park accessible only by boats. I was not interested in a long paddle. I had covered five miles in two hours drifting with the current — slow, but then I had cancelled all appointments.

At Jones Island I was greeted by a floating RV park. Power boats of all dimensions took any available parking. I squeezed in like a cat among elephants at the dock. The fee for parking and camping was five dollars. I stayed ten minutes to replenish my water and photograph tame deer. Deer have been hunted by man for thousands of years but a few generations after the killing stops, they act like brothers. I paddled off to search for a warm spot in the sun. Paradise had to be more than a roadside rest area, however envious I was of the parents I saw with their kids.

Around the island, my credit in the Bank of Good Fortune was pushed to the max as I staked a claim in the sun. I landed and threw my kayak and gear up the bank. Pulling out a bottle of elixir, a good book, my mat and sun tan lotion, I fell into nirvana. I tried to feel guilty for not hiking trails, exploring, setting up camp, etc., but I couldn't work up the steam. I laid in the sun for four hours. Kayakers passed looking for their own private spot. Other kayakers did stop down the beach.

A "stink pot" (a power boat, called such by my kayaking neighbor) was anchored in the bay. I have nothing against power boats per se. I own one myself. Access to my own island paradise 800 miles north in the same ditch (the Inside Passage) requires it. But I preferred to kayak the San Juans rather than power it, because otherwise it was inflationary: too much pleasure for too little "associated" effort. Many things are valued by their accessibility. By making this island less accessible to myself, it rose in value. I used physical exercise to arrive and received direct "associated" reward for my efforts. I was not using credit from disassociated work (money) which had little meaning to what I was doing nor would I be paying for a dead horse (credit cards). Besides, I could go where others couldn't.

I read my book. I fixed dinner and read my book and went to sleep. I departed the next morning to catch the 9:00 am shuttle. Oceans have hills. Better yet, hills that move. If you time it right, you can wait for a hill to come by, then jump on it and ride to the bottom. I had two hours to ride down the "hill" (with the tidal current) before I started riding up "hill" (against the current). Sailing out through the islands, I encountered a colony of kayakers similar to myself. My species was no longer endangered. Passing the voyagers, I exchanged salutations and picture taking.

I needed to finish my book. I looked for a warm flat spot to lay this slug. A beautiful beach was marked with signs that trespassers would be shot, fried, electrocuted, and the remains would be prosecuted. Knowing that trespass is a tort and not a crime, I sprawled in the sun and read. Nobody shot at me, but I had the feeling there was little open range in this neck of the woods.

Later that afternoon I docked at Friday harbor on San Juan Island (the island that gave the archipelago its name). I landed on an abandoned and decrepit float amidst a jungle of beautiful private floats each yearning for my last five dollar bill. I climbed a cliff with my kayak to escape with my last fin. The gods of kayaking continued to smile on me as I was late again, but so was the ferry. I struggled aboard with my wheeled tragedy like a novice seafarer who had never seen a kayak.

On board, I mused on the significance of this cruise through the magical isles. For over 20 years I have hitch-hiked, walked, rowed, rafted, kayaked, climbed, worked, studied, trained, flown, crawled, drank, crawled, and struggled across four continents (with three more to go). On the scale from one to ten, I rate most of these adventures as a three; some maybe a four. This was a three.

The experience which has the greatest possibility for success, failure, sacrifice, fulfillment, loss, self-knowledge, growth of character, and self-worth; the one experience which to me, at my decrepit age of 38, rates a pure ten on my scale of high adventure is raising a family. Never will the sacrifices be greater; the possibilities for failure so large; the self-discovery so complete; the reward so rich; the potential self-fulfillment so great. I disagree with one of my heroes who said: "Most people live lives of quiet desperation." Most people are engaged in the greatest adventure of all: parenthood (though possibly they don't realize it).

Being the major factor in a person's or persons' ultimate happiness or misery is the greatest challenge, offering the highest potential for self-knowledge and self-fulfillment; all else is a side-show.

Yet, I am into sideshows as well. From the deck of the ferry, the emerald islands shown with the brilliance of gold encrusted jewels in the late evening light.

KAYAKING NORTH OF JUNEAU
(1989)

I think I could hunt and live with animals, they are so
placid and self-contained
I stand and look at them long and long.
They do not sweat and whine about their condition,
They do not lie awake in the dark and weep for their sons,
They do not make me sick discussing their duty to God.
Not one is dissatisfied, not one is demented with the mania
of owning things,
Not one kneels to another, nor to his kind that lived
thousands of years ago,
Not one is respectable or unhappy on the whole earth.

from *Leaves of Grass*— Walt Whitman

I was kayaking the coast north of Juneau in a 17 foot rented sea kayak. Up from Stephen's Passage rollers were coming three to four feet high. Stacked on top of them were smaller waves. These waves would roll under me and smash into the 50 foot volcanic cliffs that lined the shore of the Inside Passage.

My goal was to stay close enough to land to be able to swim to shore if I flipped and couldn't Eskimo roll back over. My other goal was to make sure the waves did not make me and my kayak "one" with the volcanic rock.

Strapped to the top of my spray skirt was a waterproof tape player with earphones that played rock and roll music from a tape made by a friend. Up above in the trees on the cliff the eagles and ravens were carrying on their traditional king-of-the hill routine. The general rule is that a couple of ravens gang up on an eagle. Eagles, being larger and therefore less agile in the air, seldom get the better of a raven.

On the volcanic cliffs that reach 100 feet above the water, spruce and hemlock clung desperately to the rock. The cliffs are often battered by heavy seas pushed northward by southeasterly winds coming up the coast. They reminded me of the north coast of Kauai, Hawaii, which receives the brunt of Alaska's storms. The waves from the storms have worn down the island more than other areas, leaving steep cliffs, as the waves work inland.

These coasts north of Juneau looked freshly worn. Trees hung ready to fall at the next blow. Huge rocks lay at the bottom of them.

It was obvious from the steep and worn cliffs that I was having a good day out there. The waves were small. Having sailed the Inside Passage from Seattle to Juneau for many years, I have seen 20 foot waves blowing up Chatham Straits, sometimes backed by 100 m.p.h. winds.

Though I felt lucky for the weather, I was still impressed. I was impressed because as a Class III whitewater kayaker, I felt none too secure in my craft. I had a good Eskimo roll, but it was unproven in a sea kayak, fully loaded. When I tried a roll the day before, I had been paddling for five hours. I stopped, took out my gear, then turned over to start the roll. When the 50 degree water hit my legs that had been imprisoned for five hours below deck, they both cramped. My immediate desire to escape the craft and to forget the roll was helped by gravity. With no hip supports in the sea kayak, my knees could not hold me and I simply fell out.

By the fourth try, I made my first roll, then three more in succession. That was four in an unloaded kayak; but what about a fully loaded one, with legs trapped for hours below deck waiting to cramp at the first roll, and no one around to help? The benefits of rolling a sea kayak remained unproven to this individual.

It was a Saturday as I worked my way up the coast, but mine was the only kayak I saw. If I flipped in the bone-chilling water of 50 degrees, I felt certain I could make it to shore; if my roll failed, I might lose the kayak and the gear, but the most important asset would be saved — me. The fifty foot cliffs looked manageable as well as the two mile hike to the nearest road. Hypothermia (low body temperature) was possible but not likely because of the insulation of my wet suit. Bears were the least of my worries.

All and all, I called it a well calculated risk. I had not checked with the people I rented the kayak from about whether or not this was a good or safe place to kayak. My plans had changed at the last moment and I did not bother to consult them. It had been years since several kayakers had been drowned on this coast. I did call my wife telling her where to send the Coast Guard if I didn't call in on time.

With these thoughts in the periphery of my mind, I paddled up the coast with my friend's music smoking in my ears. I was inspired. The waves were coming up, picking up my craft gently and going on to the great wall of stone. "Born to be Wild" thundered through the earphones "firing our guns, we watched them explode into space." Man, I was rocking.

I know somewhere there is an environmental commission on natural and organic kayaking that will break my paddle, tear my spray skirt, bend my rudder, and smash my boat for paddling under the influence of electronic stimuli. But there was "power, power, thunderous working power"; Bruce Springsteen was "Standing On It" as well as many others besides. "Bad Moon Rising" echoed through my head as a 1,000 pound Sea lion broke through the ocean foam ten feet from my flagship. I know now how sea monsters are created: out of sheer terror!

Sea lions are called such because they look like a female lion, at least from the neck up. This one reminded me of a Polar bear, but I was 1,000 miles too far south for that. Finally, Sea lion clicked in my brain.

It is obvious it was not afraid of humans, yet neither did it care to dine on me or want to mate with the kayak. It slid beneath the waves with a snort and went back to eating its 15 salmon a day.

Seals, on the other hand, keep their distance from humans possibly because they are still hunted by Natives (the seals we see in the circus are actually Sea lions; true seals can't sit up on their flippers). Seal heads also stuck up out of the water, shiny and water-slickened, resembling black skulls. They reminded me of visitors from Davy Jones' lockers, "One screw-up, pal, and you are ours."

I was impressed by the waves on that coast. I found it hard to believe any inexperienced people came this way; or, in fact, any people at all — but they did. Maybe my vessel was more sound and more stable than I thought. Maybe.

I camped that night near Eagle Beach campground where two glacier-fed streams joined before they met the sea. The eagles seemed to have been run out by the local toughies — the seagulls. One of the meanest birds around, seagulls, like the raven, believe in gang warfare. You screw with one — you have to beat up a hundred of them. I once shot a seagull by mistake that was sitting next to a duck. The next thing I knew, I was surrounded by fifty screaming gulls. They decided not to pick on me other than screaming, but an eagle would have been dead meat. Eagles get great respect from humans for their good, noble human-like looks, but other birds tend to dump on them.

After paddling several miles up a rocky coastline while hanging on to the ledge of life (at least it felt that way), I camped within 50 feet of the highway. Understandably there is something demeaning in camping so near a highway, but it was a good camp site and I was tired. It looked like a hot spot for the local teenagers, considering the beer cans.

The night produced no rain, nor was there any darkness. Dusk turned to semi-darkness over a period of five hours. It was too close to the summer equinox for total night. In the twilight, Humpback whales were blowing and sounding in the distance. They are the great behemoths of the north land. Only they and killer whales feed in the protected waters of Southeast Alaska; other whales stay out in the open ocean. The protected, calmer waters of the Inside Passage allow Humpback whales to gather krill (a small shrimp) by blowing bubbles beneath the water that carry the small sea animals to the surface where the whale then scoops them up with its specialized mouth of baleen (that humans once used for skirt hoops) that filters them out. Only the sperm and killer whales hunt large animals; other whales dine on much smaller fare.

The whales and other sea mammals come from a lineage that at one time crawled out of the ocean only to return, but equipped with lungs instead of gills. Their warm-blooded system, which they also took from the land, makes them excellent denizens of the north. Some whales have blubber two feet thick which protects them in cold water and allows them to stay mobile even when salt water temperatures go

p. kadir

below 32 degrees Fahrenheit. Cold blooded animals, on the other hand, generally become sluggish in extremely cold water. Gills don't provide as much oxygen as do lungs for animals requiring warmer bodies; also gills require water to be constantly flowing through the animal which contributes to cooling.

One time when I was working on my homestead in Southeast Alaska, a whale surfaced not 50 feet from shore, spouted, and then dove. As I stood on the shore next to my place, I said, "That is why I came to Alaska: where else can I get whales in my front yard?"

Polar bears never hunt or kill penguins as they do in the comic books of Chilly-Willy. The reason is that polar bears live around the north pole and penguins only in the southern hemisphere. The difference between a penguin and seal is that seals have descended from mammals, while penguins have descended from birds. Seals push their body through the water with their tail and fins. Penguins fly through the water with their forward limbs acting as wings under water. Interestingly, sea lions inhabit both ends of the globe. An animal similar to a penguin used to live in the north but is now extinct.

The brown bears (or grizzly) of coastal Alaska vie with the polar bear for the title of the largest land carnivore. Brown bears that inhabit the area I was camping in grow to 1,800 pound and have large heads.

Polar bears can weigh as much but are often taller since they need a smaller head and longer neck to pull seals out of the ice.

Comparing the life style of the two bears, I had to side with the brown bear (actually an overgrown grizzly). He attains his size by living off the rich protein of salmon that stream inland each year to the islands of Southeast Alaska. The weather is mild on the coast, as compared to the interior and the habitat of the polar bear.

The polar bear, on the other hand, roams the Arctic ice cap most of the year trying to snag seals that come up for air in the cave like openings (blow holes) they have made in the ice. Wandering around a frozen waste land for six months a year in total darkness, always alone, waiting for days for seal to shoot up through a tube of ice does not sound like the life of Riley.

The land that the Alaskan brown bear lives in is still feeling the effects of the last ice age. When the ice that covered Southeast Alaska melted 20,000 years ago, it took considerable weight off the land. The land, with reduced, weight has been rising ever since.

That night I watched the Eagle River go by, something unusual since I was actually camped on the ocean. But in this area there are 20 foot tides which tend to hold the river back at its mouth. However, when the tide changes, the river starts to advance. Murky glacial fresh water weighs less and tends to ride on top of clearer but heavier salty ocean. As I sat at my camp, the murky glacial melt water crept by me and went on into the night.

In the morning I had my breakfast of freeze-dried chicken stew (easiest way to eat breakfast on the trail), threw my gear in the boat, and headed out. I had twenty miles to paddle to make it to the pull out point.

Having first known whitewater kayaking, I soon realized that flat water kayaking is a lot more work! I rounded bay after bay in traveling up the coast. Often I saw fishermen who had climbed down from the highway to fish off the rocks. Sometimes I asked one of them where I was. They had no better idea than I did. In my preparation for the trip I had failed to get a good map of the area; instead I had a realtor's map of Juneau. This little slip up guaranteed that if the trip wasn't dangerous enough, I had made it more so.

I paddled under full steam for most of the day. The music was rocking in my ears, the ocean waves were rocking my boat and I was rocking my arms to get water both under and past me. For some reason through the years I had become used to cold water showers and bathing. Many times I did this to reduce muscle tension and other times to cool down after a work out. I started taking regular baths in the ocean each night at my homestead a few years back. Bathing in 45 degree water gives one a profound respect for it. Many people who died from exposure or hypothermia in ocean water never had any knowledge of it to begin with. When they did get it, it was too late. I had respect for it. In fact, it scared me even as I paddled. Between me and the great unknown was a quarter inch of plastic.

I eventually rounded the corner into Berner's Bay, a place 50 miles north of Juneau, Alaska, where a large river enters the ocean. I kayaked towards the first buildings I saw. There were people on the shore, but when I pulled up there happened to be a building full of people. It was a church camp reunion I had stumbled on. The people told me I was three miles from Echo Cove where the road was. As I walked back to my kayak, I thought how interesting Alaska is. One minute I am alone kayaking in the great wilderness with no sign of man; the next minute I walk into a building with 100 people throwing a party.

I kayaked the last few miles to the end of the road. As I did I noticed people from the church group walking along the shore as fast as I could paddle. Flat water kayaking is not a high speed sport (especially against the tide.)

I beached my boat where the cars indicated a nearby road. I pulled myself out of my coffin and staggered around on shore. I was tired and my legs had been below deck for 8 hours and were stiff and sore. I waddled around for a while trying to find an outhouse. But there wasn't one so I did what everyone else did and made do in the woods. I circled back to my kayak after locating the major parking area while looking for a campsite. There was loud rock music coming from the campsite next to my boat. Cars were parked around the area and I immediately thought of teenagers drinking beer and causing havoc as I did in my misspent youth. I was surprised to notice as I walked by that it was, in fact, a family having a picnic. In my mind, I knew why this could not be a family gathering because no parents would ever allow themselves to be tortured by teenage music that was produced by musicians who looked like they had murdered their mothers.

But I was wrong about that. There was one type of family that would find their kids' music as important as theirs. This family was a Native family. I later found out that they were from the Tlingit tribe

131

of Alaskan Natives. Only would Natives let their kids exercise that much freedom around them. Non-Native parents would be bashing the boom boxes over their kids' heads. Native tradition has it that kids should not be overly disciplined when young. Life in the Alaskan wilderness was too much on the edge of existence when a Native becomes an adult. To many Alaskan tribes, children were to enjoy their youth because later heavy responsibility would fall upon them and would never lighten. Youth was a time to be carefree and unrestrained.

Whether that maxim holds true today is another question, but I appreciated seeing this Native family enjoying the same music and the fact that the elders respected the desires of the young.

A conversation started between us. I sat down and they gave me a large cup of coffee. The group was here for the anniversary of the parents. They had wanted to go seal hunting but their motor on their boat had failed.

I was glad they had offered me coffee instead of a beer. Though I feel a certain closeness to Natives because my first friend was a Navajo Indian, they have gained even less from alcohol than whites. Natives suffer as do the Irish from relatively late exposure to alcohol. Italians and Greeks, who have had thousands of years of experience with it, suffer less.

Drinking coffee with them reminded me of an incident in Peter Freuchen's *Book of the Eskimo* in which he attended an Eskimo party where the main intoxicant was coffee. The Eskimos had had such little exposure to stimulants that drinking coffee gave them the buzz that other cultures found in alcohol.

As I sat on a log trying to coherently converse with them, a little girl brought me food. They were through eating and were about to throw the rest away. I started with sandwiches, worked my way through their beans, had dessert with a brownie, and was popping marshmallows in my mouth when they left. They gave me their charcoal briquets since there was little wood for a fire.

I am not exactly sure what they thought of me since at one point the conversation trailed off. I was mostly staring into space. They packed up around me. The little girl had to ask three times for my coffee cup before I noticed she was there. When they pulled out, I had forgotten to ask for a ride down the road 17 miles to my car. I am sure they would have offered it, but I was too far gone. When they drove off, I was still popping their marshmallows into my mouth.

I suppose it was just exhaustion, but my first extended solo trip in open water in a kayak had been challenging. I crawled towards my tent and collapsed into darkness.

The next day I did my own version of a biathlon — I tried to jog the 17 miles back to my car. I made it 14 miles before I hitched a ride. Then I returned to pick up my boat.

KAYAKING WITH THE GODS
(1990)

Then out spake brave Horatius
The Captain of the Gate:
'To every man upon this earth
Death comes sooner or late;
And how can man die better
Than facing fearful odds,
For the ashes of his fathers,
And the temples of his Gods?'

Lays of Ancient Rome — Lord Macaulay

The gray water billowed around the piling. The river was high. Higher than I had ever floated the Mendenhall River which flowed four miles from the lake below the glacier to the sea. The water was near 34 degrees Fahrenheit and murky gray with glacial silt.

Placing the white-water kayak in the river, I tightened my paddling jacket at the waist, neck and hands. Underneath was a pile jacket and ⅛" long john wet suit. Wearing neoprene boots, I latched a neoprene head piece and cinched my helmet tight. Then I donned neoprene gloves.

Behind me jutted the peaks of the Alaska Coastal range and the Juneau Ice Field from which the glacier flowed. The river was smothered in the constant evergreens of Southeast Alaska's rain forest. It wasn't raining and it wasn't blowing. That's good weather in Southeast Alaska.

I slipped into the kayak, bracing with my paddle, and installed the spray-skirt that seals the craft. After watching the water pile again three feet above the river on the bridge support column, I departed. I paddled alone as usual. I did so as a transplanted white-water kayaker from the Lower 48. The flat water, kayaking mecca of Juneau, Alaska, has little white-water and fewer white-water kayakers. Flat water boating is fine, but it lacks the thrill of riding Class III rapids like a cowboy on a bucking horse.

The Mendenhall River is flat water except for a half mile stretch where the water ranges from two foot waves (Class II) to five foot standing waves with great turbulence and little escape (Class IV). I was in between, as a Class III kayaker (standing waves to four feet with a good roll required). Glacial rivers tend to rise during the day in the sun. The more the glacier melts, the higher the river. It had been a warm day, and it was a Class III river. The many rocks, debris, trees and frigid water made one rapid a Class IV.

I paddled behind a rock and floated in the back eddy. I had little chance to practice my roll or my bracing. My bracing with a paddle that kept me upright was sloppy. Also, I generally needed to roll a few times to get the feel of it. I should have driven up to Mendenhall Lake and paddled down, doing braces and rolls as I descended, instead of putting in at the bridge a half mile below the lake and immediately above the rapids. But that meant three extra miles of jogging back to my van in a wet wet suit. I was too lazy.

I shuttled into the back eddy of another rock trying to feel comfortable with my boat. I was clumsy. I had done the river earlier that summer when it was lower. It had seemed so easy that I had hardly used my paddle. But today was different.

It is not recommended to kayak alone. One kayaker often pulls another kayaker to shore with the upset kayak in tow. But had John Muir, Jack London and others waited until they had some one to go with them, they might never have gone. I had done this river several times before alone, but there had always been someone driving my van. Even that made a difference. Now there was no one.

Once I kayaked with a person on the river and we had challenged each other, ferrying across the rapids pointing up stream. I had flipped and was unable to roll up. Being a superb paddler, she had grabbed my up stretched hands and flipped me topside and guided my boat to shore. Later I flipped again, but Eskimo-rolled back up.

Now I was alone. I looked down river at the gray hay stacks formed by constriction of the water at a narrow point, piling water into large standing waves. They looked awesome to me. As I departed my rock of safety, I mumbled to myself, "I sure hope you like to swim." But I was confident. I was confident in myself that even if I had to swim, I could survive.

I hit the first haystack and shot over the top which was great fun, a good ride. After four stacks, there appeared two stacks on either side and chaos in the middle. It ate me. Whatever brace I should have done, I didn't do it; or I didn't do it right. I was upside down in 34 degree water. Reality is very real.

I tried an Eskimo roll which failed, because I tried to straighten up too soon. I went back under to try again, but in a somewhat rattled state, I did not re-seat myself. I had slid part way out of the hatch, and my second attempt was doomed. I went back under and decided to call it a night. I ejected from the frail vessel. I was alone in Class III+ glacial water hanging on to kayak and paddle.

The cold water clamped on me like a vise as I plunged through rapids gasping for breath. Even with maximum flotation gear I struggled for oxygen. The kayak and paddle twisted my arm into the shape of a pretzel. But my fears had been tempered. I was in the water, conscious, and calm enough. I could stand the temperature and rapids. For the half mile swim to calm water my gear was adequate. In that I had been prepared. Also, I was not foreign to cold water. I bath in 45 degree water at my homestead. Cold water had my deepest respect but I didn't panic in it and my defenses against it were adequate.

After rounding several bends in the river through Class II water, I saw a row of tree stumps that had been dumped in the water along the bank by a home owner. The sight sent chills through an already cold body. In my concentration, I let myself be briefly pinned by the kayak against a rock. I don't fear rocks; I bounce off of them. But trees and stumps are sieves that trap victims like spaghetti in a colander.

I positioned my kayak and paddle between myself and the long row of stumps that were dumped there to prevent erosion and kill boaters. Poking with my kayak, I kept myself away from the ugly beasts. Then came my nemesis – my *bete noir*. One or two of the stumps had rolled into the river. I could pass on river-right but I couldn't see if it was clear. If there was a tree blocking the passage, then I would be history. I could not take the risk.

Abandoning the kayak and paddle, I swam for river-left of the stump. My arms were oars and my legs threshers inching me across the swift, powerful current. I almost cleared the stump. I almost made it. But in the final moment, I was pinned like a fly to the stump of non-existence. The force of the river, making me one with that wood was unrelenting. In one to one combat, of man against the brute, terrible force of nature, there is no contest. A person may play and frolic in his craft; but in terms of pure physical force, man, stripped of his machines, is but a butterfly among the diesel engines of the earth.

In the waters cold embrace, I clung with feeble hope to the discarded hulk of a tree that was my executioner and my savior. As I dug my nails into the tree of life and death, I waited for the verdict. If negative, it meant the current was taking me under the stump to the big rapids in the sky. My immediate fear was not that I was a condemned man on death row, but if I was pushed beneath the tree, then there was no second chance. If I kept my head above water, I had ten minutes to fight for life, before succumbing to exposure. If my oxygen in-take vents were trapped below the water line, then I had ninety seconds to round out my life.

The jury was out and had gone to lunch by my estimation, but it was only five seconds in real time. The hangman had to wait. The

p. Radin

Jury of Chance had stayed my execution and granted a small reprieve. I had ten minutes to argue my case before the Gods of Adventure. Like the song says, "I was twenty-one in prison doing life without parole. Mama tried, mama tried, oh mama tried." Now, came the Court of Last Appeal.

I began the petition for my existence. I contended with all the muscle I had strengthened or developed through the years. I had briefed my case well. Barely breathing, so great was the force at my back and the pressure on my chest, my hands searched every nook and cranny for reasons that would give leverage against the dark forces of oblivion. I sensed the jury was starting to sway. I moved a millimeter, a micrometer. Encouraged, I yanked harder with the arguments of my arms and shoved desperately with the principles of legs. I screamed and shouted, but I had little air for sound. The swirling water licked and flickered with fire-like intent unmoved by appeals for clemency. The river of the prosecution did not change its course nor lessen its rage. The stump was unyielding. I had broken the Law of Kayaking: "Never paddle alone in water beyond your ability unless you are Walt Blackadar."

The Gods of Adventure heard the arguments of the prosecution:

"He is a Class III kayaker in a Class IV rapids," argued the River. "He was out of his league to begin with. He didn't practice his rolls or bracing beforehand and he was kayaking alone. Had he kayaked with another he would have been pulled to safety. Under the Laws of Safe and Hygienic Kayaking, I demand his demise."

"He didn't scout the river beforehand", gurgled the Stump from beneath the water. "If he had scouted the river, he would have seen me and been able to avoid me. But he didn't; under the Laws of Conformity he should answer with his life."

"What about Shackleton," I screamed over the thunder of the icy water.

"Shackleton who?", responded the God of Adventure.

"The Antarctic explorer," I protested, "who went on a shoe string; who made mistake after blunder. He took ponies for his journey to within 90 miles of the South Pole. He had the wrong boat built for his next trip and it was crushed and he wandered for a year on the ice with his men. You spared him and all his men even with all his errors. He broke all the laws."

"We missed him," said a God of Exploration, "but he picked off his buddy, Scott, on his return trip. Do you think you should flaunt the Laws of Safe and Homogenized Kayaking?"

"Yes," I roared above the river's rage. "As long as I am willing to pay the price for my transgressions, I can bend the rules."

"You feel you are different than the rest," mused the God of Mountaineering.

"Only so far as I accept the responsibility for ignoring the rules. I know the risks, the dangers, and the consequences of my actions. I accept the results of my actions and I am willing to give the `last full measure of devotion' for my right to cut my own trail."

"Then continue with your arguments," proclaimed the God of Kayaking.

The best argument for reprieve was that, like Shackleton, though I was not totally prepared, I was a deep pocket in endurance and survival: I was in excellent physical shape; accustomed to cold water immersion; well insulated from the cold; and had fairly well calculated the odds except for the little glitch at the end that put a hangman's noose about my neck. Shackleton may have been a klutz at planning, but he was the master of the Sudden Death Play-Off. He always brought his men home alive.

Under the contentions of my arms and the assertions of my legs, super-charged by fear, my body moved a quarter inch toward the heavens and the same distance away from watery-hell. The jurors knew I bent the rules, but one of them believed rules were meant to be broken as long as the price was paid. Slowly my body crawled from the icy womb. My spray-skirt was tangled in exhibits of debris that said I should pay for my recklessness. My legs were scrambled among the roots of pushing the envelope too far. I inched my way upward as if I were an ant escaping flames. I was a spider in a gale spinning upon the thread of life. My chilled and flattened body yearned for another chance even if I had to use the knife in my paddling jacket, leaving part of me behind: like an animal in a trap that eats its own leg to escape. I would not be denied.

Quarter inch by quarter inch I rose from the water like a person being re-born. One juror among the twelve had refused the verdict of death for my transgressions. The jury was hung, but not I. The claws of a wild beast that were once my hands aided by adrenaline pistons that were once my legs secured my reprieve. I clambered up the stump that had been condemned under the Law of the Chain Saw. As I strode with giant steps the trunk of the tree and plunged again into the swirling river to give chase to my kayak, I felt I walked with the gods; the deadly waters were now a six inch deep lukewarm puddle.

For but a flash of time, as I stepped like a behemoth across my nemesis and leaped again against my antagonist, I caught a glimpse of the great Antarctic explorer, Ernest Shackleton: the one who blazed a path to the Pole for Scott. During his third attempt at the Pole, after a desperate year of floating on an ice pack when their boat sunk, Shackleton and his men made a break for freedom in open lifeboats and landed on Elephant Island. For a minute, I understood what Shackleton saw in the difference between the two types of men who struggled ashore. Most of the men had not been with his previous expedition to within 90 miles of the Southern Pole and fell upon this first piece of land in a year in exhaustion. But the few who had been on his prior assault to the southern limits landed as if on a Sunday stroll. Even looking into the eyes of death becomes mundane if you do it long enough. For a brief moment, I thought I beheld the great Shackleton.

After being clutched by the jaws of oblivion, swimming with his cousin, mere Danger, was a trifle. Floating faster than the kayak, because I was in the water and it was on top, I regained possession of my craft. I pulled it to shore, dumped out the water, seated myself, installed the skirt, and using a flat piece of wood, paddled to the other shore. I was now past the rapids.

After jogging back to my van, I used another paddle to look for my lost one, but it was not to be found. Possibly it was mating with a tree trunk, three feet beneath the water. It was a small sacrifice to the Gods of Kayaking and Adventure. It might have been me. Even the legendary Walt Blackadar, who solo kayaked virgin Class VI rapids, had died on a tree in a river while kayaking with friends.

Once ashore I wanted to challenge the river again. It had thrashed and trashed me and I wanted revenge. But I had to settle for the desire. I was too cold and exhausted. Besides, the light was fading and the replacement paddle was inadequate. I may be crazy but I'm not stupid!

I had been a fly pinned on the Wheel of Death because I had not practiced my roll and braces; had not scouted the river; and had kayaked alone in rapids beyond my ability. Had I died I would have been sentenced to the ranks of the ill-prepared and condemned for going beyond my ability. The lesson is: always play by the rules. Or is it?

Though I failed at the primary goal of staying upright and afloat, I had been prepared. I was properly clothed and familiar with cold water immersion. At the crucial time I had made the right decision and executed it. Being in excellent shape paid off. I had failed on the primary goal maybe by being lazy, but I had successful survival methods.

Can mediocre people do heroic acts? Can Class III kayakers be heroic or do heroic acts only by beginning at Class VI?

The greatest responsibility is when we accept the consequences for our actions: when we examine the course taken and the reasons. Many people never question their actions, but take the easiest route by conforming. Hitler loved such people.

The bravest people are those who are conscious of their actions and the reasons—who question everything—and accept the outcome of taking a different path.

The average people rise above the grade when they act individually; having thought about their actions; calculating the risks and accepting them; and are willing to pay for the results. Even ordinary people loom larger than life when they refuse to drift with the current, but rather challenge it because of their hopes, ideals, and beliefs.

Though jumping into water over my head sounds reprehensible, it was a calculated risk with reasonable expectations of survival. Had I not made myself a hostage to fortune, then I might never have seen through the eyes of Shackleton.

I was proud to desire again the caldron of the dark forces. Maybe I would scout more next time. Possibly I would practice a few rolls first. But I desired to return to the gray milk-shake of death from which sprang a heightened awareness of life that let me kayak with the gods.

EPILOGUE
(1995)

In summing up twenty years of slumming in Alaska, I can say that if it is in your blood to wander frozen waste lands; live in dirty trapper cabins and frozen VW buses; suffer through strange environments far from friends and families; inflict upon yourself dangerous situations and unreasonable pain; then you will probably do it whether it makes sense or not at the time. Strangest of all, you will probably enjoy it and write a book about it.

If it is not in your blood, then you might stay at home with friends and family and read about it wishing you could inflict upon yourself such experiences and berating yourself because you didn't.

The toughest sentence for such an existence is to spend twenty years in pursuit of some new truth that you are certain the world has never touched upon only to find in the end that the same truths that guided your fathers also guide you. Yet that seems to be the folly and yet the goal of each generation: to throw away the truths of the last generation only to discover their validity after twenty years of searching.

If you can't come up with twenty years of time to endure some of experiences described herein, then you might have to settle for adventure a little closer to home but none the less as dangerous and possibly even more rewarding. If you want to live on the edge of existence, put everything on the line, throw caution to the wind; if you want to be a hostage to fortune; if you want to see how much you can endure and accomplish; if you want to push the envelope to its greatest extremes; if you want to sacrifice everything for a far off ideal; then get married. Marriage is not for the timid, it is only for the brave.

Then if you want to have the greatest feeling of accomplishment. If you want the most deprivations with the greatest possibility of reward and self-sacrifice. If you want to know self-worth and self-understanding. If you must put everything on the table and roll the dice. If you must know how good you can be and how bad you can be, then have children. Never will the sacrifices be so great, the self-awareness so potential, and the self-knowledge so complete.

If you can't stand existing on the ragged edge of life; if you are unwilling to sacrifice everything in one moment of passionate judgment; if the odds are too stiff or too steep; if you can't bring yourself to turn your life into a crap shoot; then head for Alaska and start homesteading. Some of us have to take the easier route, at least at first.

APPENDIX A
In the Tracks of Jack: A Bibliography of Jack London's Year in the Yukon and Alaska (1897-1898)

In the north, nobody talks, everybody thinks.
That is where I found myself.

— Jack London

Jack London only spent a year in the Yukon and Alaska, but his experiences and writing will forever be a part of the frozen north.

A brief description of his travels seem appropriate, since I followed many of his trails.

In July, 1897, Jack London (JL) left San Francisco on board a steamer for the Yukon Territory of Canada and the Klondike. A year later, ravaged with scurvy and broke, he returned to San Francisco, having spent $1,500 on a grubstake which never panned out.

This one year, however, was the keystone to his literary career. JL mined his experiences on the frozen banks of the Yukon River for almost 20 years. He was still bringing out ore by the cart load and the mills (the publishers) were demanding more when the "mind" shaft caved in, burying him alive at the early age of 41. JL gained his first recognition from his Yukon and Alaskan stories and his fame and name still hang upon them (as do most of his literary credentials).

One of the most important primary sources of JL's travels in the north is Fred Thompson's diary[2] which was kept by him from their departure in California to Skagway, Alaska; over the Chilkoot Pass; down the Yukon River to Steward Island; and then to Dawson City. This diary records JL's activities from leaving San Francisco on 24 July 97 to 18 Oct 97 when he parted from Thompson in Dawson City. This record is responsible for disproving that JL ran boats through Miles Rapids on the Yukon River to earn money as claimed by Irving Stone in his book on JL (see note 31).

Jack London kept his own diary[3] during his float the next year from Dawson City, Yukon Territory, to the Bering Sea at St. Michaels,

Alaska. The memoirs of Emil Jensen[4] and Marshall Bond[5] record the time spent wintering over with JL at Stewart Island and later in the Spring after break up when JL floated down to Dawson City again. JL spent most of his time during this period not mining for gold but mining "old fossils" for their Yukon and Alaskan tales. He also argued socialism.

JL's own autobiographical writings appeared in five articles soon after his return. "Through The Rapids on the Way to the Klondike"[6] describes running Miles or Box Canyon and Whitehorse Rapids on the Yukon River. Both these rapids are now under a dam, and the capital of the Yukon, Whitehorse, has lost its namesake. "Housekeeping in the Klondike"[7] describes keeping house with four men in a crowded cabin at 40 below on Stewart Island. "From Dawson to the Sea"[8] is JL's account of his 2000 mile float through Alaska. "The Gold Hunters of the North" and "The Economics of the Klondike"[9] are other articles dealing with his experiences in the north.

In John Barleycorn[10], JL briefly tells of his dealings with alcohol in the north: "As good fortune would have it, the three men in my party were not drinkers. Therefore, I didn't drink save on rare occasions and disgracefully when with other men. In my personal medicine chest was a quart of whiskey. I never drew a cork until six months afterward, in a lonely camp [Stewart River], where, without anesthetics, a doctor was compelled to operate on a man. The doctor and the patient emptied my bottle between them and then proceeded to the operation."

A letter[11] to Franklin Walker shows that JL filed in Dawson on Nov 1897 for a claim on Henderson Creek, 18 miles south of Stewart Island on the Yukon River. Mr. Hargrave's memoirs of JL in the Yukon which Charmian London (JL's second wife) relies upon in The Book of Jack London (see note 3) has never been located.

JL wrote many letters in his lifetime. Some of them deal with his experiences in the Yukon, but certainly not the majority. Therefore, the letters to Mabel Applegarth[12] (girl friend), Anna Strusky[13] (girl friend), John Cloudesley[14] (friend), Elwyn Hoffman[15] (friend), George Sterling[16] (best friend), Fred Lockley[17] (editor), and George Brett[18] (publisher) are important more for quality than quantity. Many of these letters can be found in the book Letters from Jack London[19].

JL's correspondence with former Klondike acquaintances, Clarence Buzzini, Del Bishop, Everett Barton, and W.B. Hargrave[20] casts light on his exploits in the frozen north as well.

Shedding some light on the subject of JL's wanderings in the Yukon are JL's scrapbooks and holograph manuscripts[21]. These are located at the Henry E. Huntington Library (HL) in San Marino, California.

In considering JL's time in the Yukon and Alaska and the recording of it, his fictional writings must be considered. All of JL's northern tales to some extent are based upon his experience in the Yukon and Alaska. Novels of particular note are *The Call of the Wild*[22] and *White Fang*[23] which not only describe conditions and some of JL's experiences in the far north, but are generally acknowledged by critics as some of his best works. The novel *Smoke Bellew*[24] deals with the Chilkoot Pass and the Trail of '98 as does *Daughter of the Snows*[25], but are not considered JL's better works. *Burning Daylight*[26] contains one of the finest descriptions of dogsledding. The protagonist races from Circle City, Alaska to Dyea, Alaska on the Pacific Ocean to bring back the mail over a distance of 2,000 miles round trip. The setting for this story was just before and during the gold rush of '98. The novel fails miserably as soon as it leaves Alaska.

Equally important as his novels are his short stories which are far too numerous to discuss or list here, but some of the best are "To The Man on the Trail"[27], "To Build a Fire"[28], "In a Far Country"[29], and "Love of Life"[30] (Russia's Lenin's favorite). Many of these stories give the flavor of the north as JL saw it. "Trail" tells of Christmas in a cabin on the Yukon similar to what Jack experienced and how the sourdoughs frustrate the Mounties and help another sourdough escape with his gold. "Fire" takes place on Henderson Creek where JL had his claim. "Far" describes two unfit prospectors getting cabin fever and killing each other. "Life" portrays a lost man with a broken ankle on the trail struggling to stay alive and echoes JL's float to the sea while stricken with scurvy. Interestingly, JL took the idea for this last tale from a San Francisco newspaper, years after he returned from Alaska. Many of his tales came from such sources combined with his own knowledge and experience of the land.

In considering secondary materials, it seems more appropriate to discuss the biographies that have been done on JL and then the secondary texts that helped support the works.

By far and away the best biography of JL in the north is Franklin Walker's *Jack London and the Klondike: The Genesis of an American Writer*[31]. This biography will probably be the definitive text of JL in the goldfields for many years to come. Most biographies before the date of this publication did not have access to many of JL's papers which were withheld from biographers and the public. Thus, biographies of JL fall into two classes: those pre-Walker and post-Walker. Those pre-Walker are inaccurate because of lack of research sources. Those post-Walker biographies generally have only one or two chapters on the north country which is mainly filled by quoting Walker. This bibliography, also, relies heavily upon Walker.

Because of its thoroughness and in-depth research, Walker's work has dispelled many of the myths and misconceptions created by JL and others concerning what JL did in the north.

Irving Stone's *Sailor on Horseback*[32] is probably the most controversial biography of JL. Stone first made popular the notion that JL committed suicide. This caused many of JL's papers to be withdrawn from the public and from biographers for thirty years after its printing. This caused such notable failures as Richard O'Connor's biography entitled *Jack London*[33]. However, it should be mentioned that Irving Stone's biography has done more to popularize JL than anything except JL's own writings.

Jack[34] by Andrew Sinclair is one of the better biographies of JL. However, as with most biographies of JL, the treatment of the north is short (although well annotated). Sinclair states his indebtedness to Franklin Walker for his thorough book. Charmian London's (JL second wife) two volume *The Book of JL*[35] is mostly a collection of JL's own letters, notes, and quotes. It is considered by some to be poorly organized and sentimental. However, it is still the richest published source of information on JL's life. It contains the complete text of JL's diary of his trip on the Yukon from Dawson to the Bering Sea.

Russ Kingman's book, *A Pictorial Life of Jack London*[36], is the only book dedicated to presenting Jack's life in photos. Unfortunately, the paper used in this book is not of the highest quality. Better picture resolution is possible. The text dealing with JL's travels in the Yukon is highly accurate. Photos are shown of the 1969 expedition to recover the cabin at Henderson Creek that London supposedly built near Stewart Island. Half the cabin is in Dawson and half in Oakland, California. Franklin Walker, though he dedicates his book to Russ Kingman, does not support the idea that JL spent any great time at Henderson Creek nor that he built a cabin.

The Tools of My Trade[37] by David Mike Hamilton lists the books that JL had in his library with a brief description of his notes and how they may have affected JL's life. The book is of interest to this paper if for no other reason than it contains a map of Stewart Island where JL wintered over in 1897-98. For a more through critique of JL biographies see "JL: Author in Search of a Biographer"[38] by Alfred S. Shivers.

Reaching out to the next rung on the secondary source ladder, we encounter *The JL Bibliography: A Selection of* Reports Printed in the S.F. Bay Area Newspapers: <u>1896-1967</u>[39]. Although this does not deal greatly with JL in the north, it does start in 1896 before JL left for the goldfields. The definitive bibliography on JL is *JL: A Bibliography*[40]. Containing over 4,000 entries, this large work lists JL's publications with motion pictures based on his works, including reprints and translation, as well as writings about JL in English and foreign languages. Professor Woodbridge periodically lists addenda to this bibliography in the "JL Newsletter" (see note 40). Additional bibliographical items are published in "What's New About London, Jack?"(see note 42). This is a valuable tool in locating Klondike material on JL.

It is important to list the repositories where most of the information of JL in the goldfields is located. The Henry E. Huntington Library in San Marino, California contains over 16,000 partially catalogued items related to JL. It also contains the notes from Franklin Walker's biography of JL in the Klondike. The second largest collection is at Utah State University at Logan, Utah. The Cresmer Collection at USC, L.A., CA contains the notes for JL's never completed autobiographical work which was to be entitled "Jack Liverpool" and an extensive bibliography. Special Collections Dept. of University of California, L.A., CA has Irving Stone's notes of interviews, etc. which he used to write *Sailor on Horseback*. Bancroft Library at University of California, Berkeley, has letters of an interesting exchange between JL and a Klondike acquaintance, Cornelius ('Con') Morgan Gepfert.

Other libraries with JL material are the Stuart Library of Western Americana at the University of the Pacific (Stockton, Calif.); Oakland Public Library (Oakland, Calif.); Special Collections Library at the University of Virginia (Charlottesville, Virginia); and the JL Museum at Glen Ellen, California.

Private files of importance are the Papers of Joan London, JL's eldest daughter. Also of interest is the collection of Mrs. W.R. Holman of Pacific Grove, California who purchased the material collected for years by Richard Francis as well as his pioneer bibliography.

Sources of information on what is currently happening in the world of JL are three periodicals entitled "JL Newsletter"[41], "The London Collector"[42], and "What's New About London, Jack?"[43] Also interesting is "American Book Collector"[44] which has published articles on JL during the past two decades.

Going outside JL material, we encounter the sources that many authors have used to get an idea of what the Yukon and Alaska were like in the time JL was there. Some of the better ones are *The Klondike Fever: The Life and Death of the Last Great Gold Rush*[45] and *The Big Pan Out: The Story of the Klondike Gold Rush*[46]. For a good pictorial book of the Yukon see *Klondike '98*[47]. The *Klondike Stampede*[48] is a record of a Harper's Weekly correspondent letters to that journal during the gold rush. See "Settlement and the Mining Frontier" in Volumn IX of *Canadian Frontiers of Settlement*[49] for details of mining methods in the Yukon. The writer of *Klondike Diary*[50] duplicated JL's journey over the Chilkoot and down the river to Dawson just a month after London. *God's Loaded Dice*[51] was written by a person who claimed to have met JL in Dawson. *Three Years in the Klondike*[52] is a readable text of the Klondike experience. *The Trail of the Gold Seekers*[53] is the account of an attempt to reach the Yukon overland through Canada.

Other interesting, more popular present day readings are *Sourdough Sagas*[54], *Klondike Kate*[55], and *Soapy Smith in Skagway*[56]. To get a taste of what JL could have done had he had the health and the inclination, read *Tales of A Norwegian Cheechako: Greenhorn with a Gold Pan*[57]. This story relates how a person with little knowledge of the wilderness or gold panning conquered the wilderness and came out with a fortune (only to blow it in one month in San Francisco).

Also, for interesting articles on the Yukon in 1898 concerning the first explorers and prediction of starvation in 1898 in Dawson see National Geographic Magazine "The NW Passes to the Yukon", "Overland Routes to the Klondike", and "The Future of the Yukon Gold Fields"[58].[59]

For present day glimpses of the Yukon and the route to the goldfields, "Rafting Down the Yukon"[60] is an excellent article with photos on almost exactly the same route taken by JL. The country has changed little. The later film of this story, entitled "Yukon Passage"[61], is well done and gives a good idea of how it was in '98.

Another good film of the Klondike era is "City of Gold"[62], a documentary on the past and present of Dawson City. It sums up the gold rush thusly: "In '97 there was starvation. In '98 there was everything money could buy. In '99 it was over." The best commercial film made on a JL's northern tale is MGM's "Call of the Wild" with Clark Gable (1932); although it does not always hold the story line.

For those tired of books and wishing to trace the route of JL themselves, a ship of the Alaska Marine Highway[63] leaves Bellingham, Washington [the ferry system moved its southern terminus 90 miles north of Seattle in 1989] every Friday, bound for Southeast Alaska[64] and Skagway[65]. At Skagway, thousands of people climb the Chilkoot Trail every year which is now maintained and protected by the National Park Service[66]. After the pass, those wishing to canoe from Lake Bennett to Whitehorse may rent canoes in Whitehorse, Yukon Territory[67]. However, the more popular (and easier) route is from Whitehorse to Dawson[68]. This section of the Yukon is primitive and echoes the past well. For 500 miles the Yukon is a museum of deserted towns and cabins, left intact when the trade moved off the river to the road in the 1950's.

Thousands of people float this section of the river each year (most of them Germans). People doing this great adventure can stop at Stewart Island and Burien Store's where JL wintered over in '98. They may wish to search for Henderson Creek 18 miles down stream from Stewart Island where supposedly JL built a cabin to work his claim. At Dawson City half of the cabin and a re-built other half can be seen. A sternwheeler now runs the 100 miles between the historic Dawson City and Eagle, Alaska. The float down to Eagle, Alaska is also a good trip, although it is harder to rent a canoe because of crossing an international border. The float from Eagle to Circle City of 200 miles through Yukon-Charlie National Park is enjoyable[69]. The remaining 1000 mile float to the Bering Sea is possible, but few people do the entire stretch each year. Also, most people near the Yukon delta portage over into the Kuskoquim River basin to end their trip at the mouth of the Kuskoquim River.

Though this paper avoids critiques of JL writings, one should be mentioned. This is Jack London[70] by Earle Labor. He was the first person to give a lecture on JL at a university (some fifty years after JL died). It seems the literary world must finally give the devil his due, because the rest of the world refuses to forget Jack London.

APPENDIX B
Chronology of Jack London's Year in the Yukon and Alaska

1896

August 17   Strike on the Klondike River, Yukon, Territory, Canada.

1897

July 14   Excelsior docks at San Francisco (first news of gold strike to the continental U.S.).

July 24   Umatilla departs San Francisco with JL. JL changes to *City of Topeka* at Port Townsend, Wash.

August 2   Arrives Juneau, Alaska.

August 3   Departs Juneau by canoe for Skagway and Dyea.

August 7   Arrives at Dyea. Rented boat and paddled six miles to end of navigation on Dyea river. [Read: "A Daughter of the Snows"]

August 12   Finnegan Point (end of navigation).

August 14   14 miles to the summit from this point.

August 21   Sheep camp. (Read: "Which Men May Remember", "Trust").

August 30   The Scales.

August 31   Crater Lake. Nine miles to Lake Lindeman.

September 8   Lake Lindeman. Builds boats to float the Yukon. (Read: "The One Thousand Dozen", "The Sun Dog

Trail").

September 12	Sets sail and departs. Six miles to Lake Bennett.
September 22	Lake Bennett. Forty-three miles of sailing and rowing across Bennett, Nares, Tagish, and Marsh Lake to the Sixty Mile Stretch of the Yukon River.
September 24	Miles Canyon and Whitehorse Rapids. (Read: 'Through the Rapids on the Way to the Klondike.')
September 26	Lake LaBarge. Thirty miles across. (Read "The Argus of the North"; "Cremation of Sam McGee" by Robert Service).
October 2	The Thirty Mile Stretch of the Yukon River.
October ?	Five Finger Rapids. 190 miles from the start of the Thirty Mile Stretch, approximately.
October 6	Fort Selkirk
October 9	Stewart River. 140 miles from Five Finger Rapids, approximately.
October 16	Leaves for Dawson the first time to file claim. 80 miles to Dawson.
October 18	Arrives Dawson.
November	River freezes.
December 3	Leaves Dawson for Stewart Island.
December 7	Arrived Stewart Island second time. (Read: "A Day's Lodging", "The Son of the Wolf").

1898

May	Leaves Stewart Island for the second time and floats down to Dawson City

June 8	Leaves Dawson by boat (21 day float)
June 30	Arrives St. Michaels on the Bering Sea
August	Arrives in San Francisco in early August.

APPENDIX C
Notes

0 Money to start a new enterprise. Originally a mining term

1 "The Cremation of Sam McGee." Robert Service

2 Jack London's Yukon Diary. Jack London. HL

3 Emil Jensen Manuscript Memoirs. HL (copy). Unpublished

4 Marshall Bond Manuscript Memoirs. Marshall Bond, Jr. HL (copy). Unpublished

5 "Through The Rapids On The Way To The Klondike." JL. Home Magazine, June 1899

6 "House Keeping In the Yukon." JL. Harper's Bazaar, 15 Sept 1900.

7 "From Dawson To The Sea." JL. Buffalo Express, 4 June 1899.

8 "The Gold Hunters of the North." Revolution and Other Essays. JL. New York: MacMillian Co., 1910.

9 "The Economics of the Klondike." JL. The American Monthly Review of Reviews, Jan 1900.

10 John Barleycorn. JL. New York: Greenwood Press. 343.

11 Letter of J.D. Dines, Mining Recorder, to Frank Walker, August 31, 1954, enclosing a copy of JL's application for a placer mining claim on 5 Nov 1897. Franklin Walker Collection. HL.

12 Mabel Applegarth, letters from JL. HL.

13 Anna Strundky, letters from JL. HL.

14 Cloudesley John correspondence. HL.

15 Elewyn Hoffman, letters from JL. HL.

16 George Sterling, letters from JL. HL.

17 Fred Lockley papers, editor of Pacific Monthly. HL.

18 George Brett of MacMillen Co., letters from JL. HL.

19 Letters from Jack London. Edited by King Hendricks and Irving Shepard. London: MacGibbon & Kee, 1966.

20 Correspondence of Klondike acquaintances of JL: Clarence, Buzzini, Del Bishop, Everett Barton, & W.B. Hargrave. HL.

21 Basic collection of holograph manuscripts and JL scrapebooks. HL.

22 The Call of the Wild. JL. London: Octopus Books, 1987.

23 White Fang. JL. London: Octopus Books, 1987.

24 Smoke Bellew. JL. London: Readers Library Publishing Co., 1900.

25 Daughter of the Snows. JL. Philadelphia: J.B. Lippinatt, Co., 1902.

26 Burning Daylight. JL. New York: MacMillian Co., 1910.

27 "To The Man on the Trail." JL. Warsaw: Iskry, 1986.

28 "To Build a Fire", To Build a Fire And Other Stories JL. New York: Century Co., 525-534.

29 "In a Far Country", Tales of the West. JL. New York: Jameson Books, 1987.

30 "Love of Life", Love of Life And Other Stories. JL. New York: Macmillian Co., 1906.

31 JL and the Klondike: The Genesis of an American Writer. Franklin Walker. Liverpool: C. Tinling & Co. Ltd., 1966.

32 Jack London, Sailor On Horseback. Irving Stone. Garden City, N.Y: Doubleday & Co., 1938.

33 Jack London. Richark O'Connor. Boston: Little Brown & Co., 1964.

34 Jack. Andrew Sinclair. New York: Harper & Row, 1977.

35 The Book of JL, 2 vols. Charmian London. N.Y: Century, 1921.

36 A Pictorial Life of Jack London. Russ Kingman. N.Y: Crown Publishers, 1979.

37 The Tools of My Trade: The Annotated Books in Jack London's Library. David Mike Hamilton. Seattle and London: University of Washington Press, 1986.

38 "JL: Author in Search of a Biographer." Alfred S. Shivers. American Book Collector, XII (March, 1962), 25-27.

39 A JL Bibliography: A Selection of Reports Printed in the San Francisco Bay Area Newpapers: 1896-1967, M.A. Thesis. Tony Bubber. San Jose State College, 1968.

40 Jack London: A Bibliography. Hensley C. Woodbridge, John London, and George H. Twensy. Georgetown, Calif: Talisman Press, 1906[?]. Enlarged edition, Millwood, N.Y; Kraus Reprint Corp., 1973.

41 JL Newsletter. Ed., Hensley C. Woodbridge. Carbondale,Ill: So. Illinois U. Library.

42 The London Collector. Ed., Richard Wiederman (Grand Rapids, Michigan 49506).

43 What's New About London, Jack? Ed., David H. Schlottmann (929 South Bay Rd., Olympia, Wash.).

44 American Book Collector. Ed., W.B. Thorsen (1822 School St., Chicago, Ill.), which has published articles on JL during the past two decades; see especially "JL Special #" of American Book Collector, XVII (Nov., 1966).

45 The Klondike Fever: The Life and Death of the Last Great Gold Rush. Pierre Burton. New York, 1958.

46 The Big Pan Out: The Story of the Klondkide Gold Rush. Kathyn Winslort. New York: Norton, 1951.

47 Klondike '98. Ethel Becker & E.A. Gegg's. Portland, Oregon: Binford and Mort, 1949.

48 The Klondike Stampede. Jappan Adney. New York: Harper, 1900.

49 Settlement and the Mining Frontier in Vol. IX of Canadian Frontiers of Settlement. Toronto, 1936.

50 Klondike Diary. Robert B. Mekill's. Portland, Ore: Beattie, 1949.

51 God's Loaded Dice: Alaska 1987-1930. E.P. Morgan. Caldwell, Id: Caxton Printers, 1948.

52 Three Years in the Klondike. Jeremiah Lynch. London: E. Arnold, 1904.

53 Trail of the Gold-Seekers. Hamlin Garlands. New York: Macmillan Co., 1899.

54 Sourdough Sagas. Herbert L. Heller. Cleveland: World Publishing Co., 1967.

55 Klondike Kate. Lucia Ellis. New York: Hastings House, 1962.

56 Soapy Smith in Skagway. (Info not available at this time).

57 Tales of a Norweign Cheechako: Greenhorn with a Gold Pan. (Info not available at this time).

58 "The NW Passes to the Yukon", "Overland Routes to the Klondike", "The Future of the Yukon Goldfields." National Geographic Magazine. Vol. IX, 4: 105., 1898.

59 "The Alsek River's Turnback Canyon and Mt. Blackadar", Salt Lake Tribune. Michael P. Dixon. 14 Oct. 84, Sec. T: 1.

60 "Rafting Down the Yukon", National Geographic Magazine. 148: 830., Dec., 1975.

61 "Yukon Passage." Produced by National Geographic Magazine, 1977.

62 "City of Gold." (videorecording). National Film Board of Canada. Sandy Hook, Conn: Real Images, 1981.

63 Alaska Marine Highway. For information write AMH, Box 25535, Juneau, Ak. 99802-5535. Or call (907) 465-3941.

64 For an account of sailing the Inside Passage see: "Inside Passage." Michael P. Dixon. Salt Lake Tribune: Salt Lake City, Utah, Jan. 6, 1991, page W3.

65 For information write: Skagway Chamber of Commerce, Skagway, Ak., or National Park Service, Washington, D.C.

66 For information on hiking the Chilkoot Trail write: National Park Service, Skagway, Alaska.

67 For information on renting canoes or gor guided trips write: Chamber of Commerce, Whitehorse, Yukon Territory, Canada.

68 See: Canoes Routes of the Yukon. (Info not available at this time.)

69 See: "Success or Failure" (unpublished). Michael P. Dixon. Petersburg, Alaska: Dixon Archives, 1987.

70 Jack London. Earle labor. N.Y: Twayne Publishers,1974.

APPENDIX D
A List of Guides and Outdoor Travel Opportunities

The complete addresses and phone numbers of the outfitters and guides is available from the Alaska Wilderness Recreation and Tourism Association at POB 22827 Juneau, Alaska 99802, phone (907) 463-3038 or fax (907) 463-3280 .

The members listed here do not necessarily endorse or oppose any of the views expressed in this book. Except where indicated the area code for the following numbers in Alaska is (907):

64th Parallel 479-8300
7 Bridges Boats & Bikes 479-0751
A Cloudberry Lookout Bed and Breakfast . 479-7334
ABEC's Alaska Adventures 457-8907
ADF&G Watchable Wildlife 267-2149
      /Nongame Program
Admiralty Island Sightseeing 789-4786
Adventure Alaska Tours, Inc. 248-0400
Adventure Tourism 274-3038
Adventures & Delights 276-8282
Afognak Wilderness Lodge 486-6442
Akhiok-Kaguyak, Inc. 377-2770
Alagnak Lodge, Inc. 916-487-6198
Alaska Angling 719-471-2984
      (formerly Angler's Covey)
Alaska Applied Sciences, Inc. 586-1426
Alaska Bed and Breakfast 586-2959
Alaska Bicycle Tours 766-2869
Alaska Cruises (formerly Outdoor Alaska) 225-6044
Alaska Discovery, Inc. 780-6505
Alaska Division of Tourism 465-2012
Alaska Dreams 479-7712
Alaska Leading Edventures 747-4777

160

Alaska Llama Treks 376-3643
Alaska Mountaineering & Hiking 272-1811
Alaska Native Tourism Council 274-5400
Alaska Natural History Expeditions 337-0608
Alaska Nature Walks 767-5522
Alaska Northwest Publishing Co. 206-774-9009
Alaska Passages 772-3967
Alaska Raft Adventures 683-2215
Alaska Rainforest Tours 463-3466
Alaska Retreat 733-2414
Alaska River Adventures 595-1422
Alaska River Journeys 349-2964
Alaska Sail & Paddle 465-4290
Alaska Sightseeing Tours 206-441-8687
Alaska Sojourns 376-2913
Alaska State Parks 762-2602
Alaska Tails of the Trail 455-6469
Alaska Tolovana Adventures 272-2255
Alaska Travel Adventures 789-0052
Alaska Up Close 789-9544
Alaska Welcomes You! 349-6301
Alaska Wilderness Studies 786-1122
Alaska Wildland Adventures 783-2928
Alaska Wildtrek 235-6463
Alaska's Leading EdVentures 747-4777
Alaska-Denali Guiding, Inc. 733-2649
Alaskan Solitude 697-2252
Alaskan Wilderness Sailing Safaris 835-5175
Allen Marine, Inc. 747-8100
Anadyr Adventures 835-2814
Angstadt, Inc. 610-373-3112
Arctic 7 Rentals 479-0751
Arctic Air Guides Flying Service 442-3030
Arctic Circle Educational Adventures 442-3509
Arctic Poppy Bed & Breakfast 258-7795
Arctic Treks 455-6502
Around The Bend, Unlimited 474-0778
Back Country Logistical Services 457-7606
Bernholz & Graham 561-4488
Beyond Boundaries Expeditions 916-426-3168

Black Fox Lodge 733-1392
Black Spruce Lodge 895-4668
Brabazon Expeditions 747-3826
Branch River Air Service .... -246-3437
Brightwater Alaska, Inc. 344-1340
Bud's Guiding Service 697-2252
Canoe Alaska 479-5183
Cathcart Ltd. 258-6240
Center for Alaskan Coastal Studies, Inc. ... 235-6667
Chelatna Lake Lodge, Inc. 243-7767
Chilkat Guides Ltd. 766-2491
Choice Marine Charters 243-0069
Christopher Beck & Associates 272-6365
Chugach National Forest: 224-3374
    Seward Dist.Ranger
Clearwater Outdoor Services 457-7189
Colorado Outward Bound School ....
Cooperative Adventures 747-5749
Copper Oar 279-8924
Denali Backcountry Lodge 683-2594
Denali National Park 683-2290
    Wilderness Centers, Ltd.
Denali Parks Resorts 683-2215
Denali Wilderness Lodge 479-4000
Discovery Voyages 424-7602
Eagle River Center & Coop ....
Eagle River Raft Trips 333-3001
Ecotourism Associates 586-9068
Equinox Wilderness Adventures 274-9087
Eruk's Wilderness Float Tours 345-7678
F/V Cathy J 945-3518
Fantasy Ridge Alpinism, Inc. 303-728-3546
Favorite Bay Inn 788-3378
Fish and Wildlife Service (U.S.) 786-3357
Fishing and Flying 424-3324
Frontier Flying Service, Inc. 474-0014
Gary Gray, Registered Guide 784-3451
Gastineau Guiding Company 586-2666
Glacier Bay Adventures 697-2442
Glacier Bay Sea Kayaks 697-2257

Glacier Guides, Inc. 697-2252
Gold King Creek, ... 459-8288
    The Alaska Range, of course ....
Great Alaska Fish Camp & Safaris 262-4515
Gustavus Inn at Glacier Bay 697-2254
Gustavus Marine Charters 697-2233
Gusto Tours & Charters 697-2416
Harmony Point Wilderness Lodge 234-7491
Hatcher Pass Lodge & Ski School 745-5897
Honey Charters 344-3340
Hook-M-Up Tours 675-4376
Icy Strait Adventures 239-2255
Iniakuk Lake Lodge 479-6354
Kachemak Bay Wilderness Lodge 235-8910
Kantishna Roadhouse 1- 800-942-7420
Kenai Fjords Tours Ltd. 276-6249
Kenai Fjords Wilderness Lodge 224-5271
Kenai Peninsula Guided Hikes 288-3141
Kenai Peninsula Hike 'n' Lunch Tours 283-5015
Kennicott Glacier Lodge 258-2350
Kennicott-McCarthy Wilderness Guides ....
Ketchum Air Service 243-5525
Keystone Raft & Kayak Adventures, Inc. .. 835-2606
Kodiak Nautical Discoveries 486-5234
Kuskokwim Economic 675-4418
    Development Council
Lisianski Inlet Lodge 735-2266
Little Delta Lodge 274-8614
Lower Yukon Economic 438-2233
    Development Council
Marine Adventure Sailing Tours 789-0919
Merlin Charters 586-2701
Mike Cusack's King Salmon Lodge 277-3033
Moose John Outfitters 783-2129
Mountain Trip 345-6499
Mystic Lake Lodge/Alaska Trophy Hunts 745-3168
NANA 265-4139
Natchik Charters 835-5042
National Bank of Alaska 265-2134
National Outdoor Leadership School 745-4047

Nature Alaska Tours 488-3746
Nichols Expeditions 801-259-7882
North Country Outfitters 883-5506
Northern Lights Snowmobile Tours 495-1700
Northwest R & I 224-5844
Northwestern Aviation 442-3525
Nova Riverrunners Inc. 745-5753
Nuliaq Alaska Charters 474-0040
Ocean Explorers 345-6126
Olga Bay Lodge, Inc. 486-5373
Orion Outfitting 376-2913
Osprey Alaska Inc. 595-1265
Osprey Expeditions 683-2734
Otter Cove B&B 735-2259
Ouzel Expeditions, Inc. 783-2216
Packer Expeditions 983-2544
Peace of Selby, Inc. 672-3206
Pelican Charters 735-2460
Picnic Cove Charters 747-3978
Pioneer Outfitters 778-2266
Prince William Sound Books 835-5175
Ptarmigan Lake Lodge 456-6967
PWS Express 835-5807
R-W's Fishing 266-7888
Rainy Pass Lodge 349-4976
Raven Charters & Berth and Breakfast 835-5863
Red Onion Saloon/ 983-2413
    Madam Jan's Gold Panning Camp
Riversong Lodge 274-2710
Rock Rest Adventures 919-542-5502
Rust's Flying Service 243-1595
Seaview Charters 835-5115
Silvertip Guide Service 293-2326
Sitka's Secrets 747-5089
Sockeye Cycle 766-2869
Sourdough Outfitters 692-5252
Southeast Alaska Ocean Adventures 747-5011
Spectrum Sciences 276-4408
Spirit Charters 235-3978
Spirit Mountain Cabins 277-8059

Spirit Walker Expeditions, Inc. 607-2266
St. Elias Alpine Guides 277-6867
Stan Stephens Charters, Inc. 835-4731
Starbuck Charters 735-2266
Stephan Lake Lodge 696-2163
Susitna Riverover Charters 478-4330
Swiss Alaska Inn 733-2424
Talkeetna Camp and Canoe 733-2267
TAQUAN AIR 225-1010
Tawah Trading Co., Inc. 274-0783
The Blue Heron Inn 784-3287
The Boat Company 407-832-8845
The River Wrangellers 822-3967
The RiverHouse B&B 766-2060
The Village Inn, Inc.- Valdez 277-8800
The Wilderness Society 272-9453
Tok River Outfitters 883-4092
Tolovana Hot Springs, Ltd. 455-6706
Tongass Kayak Adventures 772-4600
Tongass National Forest: 747-6671
Tooliwak Expeditions . . . . 322-0572 (Cellular)
Tours on the Kenai 260-3369
Trails to the Last Frontier 822-5054
Trailside Discovery 274-5437
Tri River Charters 733-2400
Tsaina Lodge/Chugach 835-3500
       Wilderness Outpost Inc.
Tutka Bay Lodge 235-3905
U of A Fairbanks, School of Management . 474-6525
Ultima Thule Outfitters 344-1892
Ultimate RIvers 346-2193
Umiat Enterprises, Inc. 488-2366
USF&WS, Alaska Maritime NWR 235-6546
Uyak Bear Reserve 487-2122
Valdez Harbor Boat & Tackle Rental 835-5002
VanGo Custom Tours & Alaska Places 455-6499
Vern Humble Alaska Air Adventure 349-4976
Viapan Camp 583-2152
Water Ouzel Outings 772-3101
Wavetamer Kayaking 486-2604

Whalers Cove Lodge 788-3378
Wilderness Air, Inc. 486-8101
Wilderness Alaska 345-3567
Wilderness: Alaska/Mexico 479-8203
Wilderness Birding Adventures 694-7442
Wilderness Enterprises 488-7517
Wilderness Swift Charters 463-4942
Winter King Charters 424-7170
World Explorer Cruises 415-393-1565
Wrangell "R" Ranch 345-1160
Your Wilderness Connection Ltd. 463-6788
Yukon River Tours 452-7162

ACKNOWLEDGMENTS

Author thanks Jerry Dixon, Darcy Dixon, Ron Watters, Kathy Daly, Jim Brock, and Bob Blackadar for being the source of the first story he published. Rod Dixon, Todd Dixon, and Carleen Dixon all helped in some way to this book. The professors Alan Cheuse and Deborah Kaplan helped edit the author's Master's thesis. Greg, Rad, Sue Beach, George Reifenstein, Chuck Stotts, Don Bullock, Deborah Dixon and Jim Hewes are acknowledged for their contribution to the adventures herein. The author thanks Bruce Paige, Peter Mickelson, Virginia Buchanan, Tamera Edwards, Gary Madderome, Peggy Kadir and Ron Watters for their advice regarding the text.

The author acknowledges John Powell, Mel Kelso, Bruce Decker, Paula May, Crissie Dixon, Bob Seidman and Gary Dmoch for their experiences with the author which influenced the stories. The author thanks Paul Andrews, Christina Klein, Peter Anderegg and Sam Sanders for editing, indexing and graphics.

The author thanks Jerry Dixon, Peggy Kadir, Jim Asper, Rod Dixon and others for their drawings and paintings.

The author acknowledges Jonathan Bliss, Chuck Stotts, and the great Colman McCarthy for use of their quotes.

The author acknowledges Dick Nelson, Frank Pignanelli, Brita Rice, Bonnie Westland, Dan Savone, Mark, Sven, Ernie, Doug, Curt Bill, Charlie, Marcie, Norma, Elizabeth, Sharon, John, Bob, Will, Garth, George Brererton, Farrell Brown, Mike Crosby, Terry Slater,

John Costandi, Jan Baron, Stuart Baptista, Kim Balls, Gary Bliss, Fred Butler, Beth Campbell, Jane Manning, Randee Drake, York McDowell, Ray Preston, Ben Bishop, Dawn Dinwoodie, Bob Dobrynski, Dave Dawson, Barbara Holian, Stan Hojt, Grandma Lossle, Art and Muriel Dalley, Ray Justice, Dick and Miriam Jackson, Art Johnson, Pam O'Brien, Peggy Kadir, Mona Kadir, Tariq Kadir, Benan and Sylvia Kadir, Hoobie, Bonnie and Dick Dalley, Katie Haven, Rick Mercer, Jack Stone, Jim Morris, Billy Motes, Doug Peques, Fisher Rhymes, Pat and Harold Stolpe, Gladys Seeds, Rick Vox, Stan Whittaker, Terry and Sandy Wolf, Mahmood and Bedoor Suleiman, Robert, Leimoni, Zainab, Milo George and Barbara Haralovich, Alex, Tesa, Max, Victor, Lou Cafeo, Grant Webber, Ruby and Jerry Balls, Tammy Balls, Diane Downs, Tomas Delgadillo, Brita Rice, Allen Rose, Mark Holina, Tina Smiley, Joe Powers, Fred Hiltner, Carl and Helen Morris, Kelvin Avery, Skitter Watters, the Borghetto family, Beth Taylor, Pinkie Turner, Kate Ginzler, Bonnie Herbold, Jenny Eberle, Eva Barrett, Bruce and Verleen Belden, Art Bloom, Roy Darke, Goodhue Livingston, Bill Decker, Deborah Dixon, Kipp, Pyper, Gloria Dixon, Shaun, Michelle, Sally and Warren Dorbeck, Ned and Sherri Dearborn, O'Neil Del Giudice, Paul Grant, Carmen Huamanchumo, Grandma Hoppe, Mark Hutson, Phil Morris, Bob Jacobs, Nancy Lethcoe, Ron Karpick, Kybor Barnes, Randall and Robert Lauderdale, Betty Lisle, David Lisle, Joe and Sandy Morris, Bob and Jenny Morris, Todd and Sarah Rhodes, Barbara and Jim Full, Susan Minola, Gus Nelson, Dana Olson, Von Osgathopre, Fabio Buzzi, Kim and Barbara Turley, Sid, Jack, Nels, Beulah Payne, Frank Russell, Carol Shoemaker, Joni Gates, Denae, Dela Suleiman, Tony Strong, Sven Johasson, John and Joan Loosle, Roger Porto, Carol Sikelee, the great Harold R. Summers, Phillipino Pete, Suzanne Bauers, Dermot and Dory O'toole, Don and Rose McGee, Bob Pegues, Geoff Pegues, Dale and Diane Zeal, Al Brown, Karleen, Fada Murphy, Rosy Floresca, Lee and Rita White, Frank Giardino, Myron Klein, Grant Webber, Ray Matichowski, "Shakey" Acres, Beaver, Rick Nybeck, Dave Malgram, Jim Beedle, Pete McMahon, Ray Tee, Baggins, Bernie Lyshol, George Brererton, Tom Streeper, Sr., Vicki James, Mary Ann Day, Terry and Sandy Wolf, Ben Bishop, Stan Hjort and many others who had all somehow shared in my adventure of life.

I would like to thank my son Matthew for doing such a good job of raising me.

INDEX

Symbols

C

L

M

ABOUT THE AUTHOR

Michael P. Dixon was born on April 9, 1950, in Salt Lake City, Utah, and is an American citizen. When he earned a B.A. in History from the University of Utah in 1972 he went to work on cruise ships in Alaska as a waiter. When he received his J.D. degree from Gonzaga Law School in 1979 he started working in the engine room on the same ships. When he passed the bar exam, he became a purser. When he received his M.A. in English, he hoped to go on deck. To paraphrase Shakespeare, "though this may seem like madness, yet there is method in it."

He works in Alaska on cruise ships and lives on his homestead in the Alaskan wilderness.

Michael Dixon had hitchhiked across three continents by the age of 21. He supported himself as an illegal worker in Europe for a year while studying languages. He has had his residence in the Alaska wilds for the last 20 years. Mike is an avid kayaker, hiker, climber, camper adventurer and day dreamer.

He published his first article in 1983.

If you would like another copy of this book please send a check or money order for $13.95 plus $2.00 for postage and handling to

Dixon Paperback Co.
POB 240804
Douglas, Alaska 99824-0804
(907) 789-3898

or to order by credit card call:

BookCrafters, Inc.
at
(800) 879-4214

Order Form: *Alaska Bound*

Name: _____

Mailing Address: _____

City: _____ State: _____

Postal Code: _____ Country: _____

Copies ordered: _____ × $13.95=$_____

Postage and Handling: $2.00

Total Enclosed: $_____

Please enclose check or money order.

In a quiet residential neighborhood outside a large metropolitan city lives a woman with an extraordinary gift. She is performing miracles.

She has cured cancer, hepatitis, infertility and hundreds of other diseases. I have verified many of these miracles. This book is about her, the people she has healed and the force behind her miracles.

This book will introduce you to a power that you may tap into for your won health and well being. I believe the most powerful tool to cure disease is modern day medical technology combined with the healing power. With this combination there is no disease that cannot be cured, no illness that cannot be overcome. This power can be harnessed for the benefit of all mankind. I believe it is time.

—Todd Dixon, M.D.

The Book is :   *Miracles of the Healing Power*
POB 21665
Albuquerque, NM 87111
or phone (800) 381-5454

✂ -

Order Form: *Miracles and the Healing Power*

Name: _____

Mailing Address: _____

City: _____ State: _____

Postal Code: _____ Country: _____

- -

Copies ordered: _____ × $17.95=$_____

Postage, tax and handling included!
A cashier's check or money order will speed
your order

The Los Angeles Daily News gives NEVER TURN BACK their highest rating:

Four Stars: ★★★★

"It's the best thing to come across this reviewer's desk in recent memory. "

—Brett Pauly

If you enjoy reading about Alaska and wilderness adventures, then you'll love NEVER TURN BACK by Ron Watters. The book tells the gripping and compelling life story of Walt Blackadar, one of the outdoor world's most famous and controversial personalities. At the age of 49, he rose to fame after making a solo kayak journey down the treacherous rapids of Turnback Canyon on the wild Alsek River in Canada and Alaska.

The San Francisco Chronicle
Says: *"Bully for Watters!"*

"Magnificent . . . told with sparkling clarity . . . truly inspirational."

—William Bushnell, *Eclectic Book Reviews*, Library Research Associates, New York

Price $14.95. Available From: The Great Rift Press, 1135 East Bonneville, Pocatello, ID 83201.

Call Toll Free: 1-800-585-6857